About the Author

Dr Kevin Donnelly AM

Since first warning about the dangers of political correctness during the early 1990s, Kevin has established a reputation as one of Australia's leading conservative commentators and authors fighting against cultural-left ideology and groupthink that is poisoning society and stifling free and open debate.

Political correctness (rebadged as being Woke) denies the ability to reason and be impartial as knowledge, supposedly, is a social construct and all relationships are based on privilege and power. In opposition, Kevin champions the strengths and benefits of Western civilisation and a liberal education dedicated to what the poet T. S. Eliot describes as "the preservation of learning, for the pursuit of truth, and in so far as men are capable of it, the attainment of wisdom".

Kevin also champions the West's Judeo-Christian heritage and ongoing traditions that underpin and enrich our language, literature, music, art, political and legal systems and way of life, which are being undermined by a rainbow alliance of neo-Marxist, postmodern, post-colonial theories.

As well as appearing on Sky News, Kevin has been published by *The Australian*, *The Herald Sun*, *The Daily Telegraph*, *Quadrant Online*, *The Spectator Australia*, *The Catholic Weekly* and the UK-based *The Conservative Woman*. His previous publications include: *Why our schools are failing*, *Dumbing Down*, *Australia's Education Revolution*, *Educating your child: it's not rocket science*, *Taming the black dog*, *The Culture of Freedom*, *How Political Correctness is Destroying Australia*, *How Political Correctness is Destroying Education*, *How Political Correctness Is Still Destroying Australia*, *A Politically Correct*

Dictionary and Guide, Christianity Matters In These Troubled Times, Why Christianity Is Good For Us, Cancel Culture And The Left's Long March and *The Dictionary Of Woke.*

Kevin taught for 18 years in Victorian government and non-government secondary schools and has also been a member of state and national curriculum bodies, including the Victorian Board of Studies and the federally funded Discovering Democracy programme. In 2014 Kevin co-chaired the review of the Australian National Curriculum for the Commonwealth Government.

Dr Donnelly is a senior fellow at the Australian Catholic University's PM Glynn Institute. In the 2016 Queen's Birthday Honours List, Kevin was appointed as a Member of the Order of Australia for services to education. Kevin can be contacted via email at *kevind@netspace.net.au* or his website *kevindonnelly.com.au*

Once knowledge is equated with ideology, it is no longer necessary to argue with opponents on intellectual grounds or to enter into their point of view. It is enough to dismiss them as Eurocentric, racist, sexist, homophobic – in other words, as politically suspect.

Christopher Lasch, *The Revolt Of The Elites And The Betrayal Of Democracy*

By destroying the credibility of traditional ways of practising faith, through feasts, rituals, and displays, they created a vacuum. Man seeks ecstasy and transcendence, and if he cannot find it in church, he will look for them elsewhere.

Adam Zamoyski, *Holy Madness: Romantics, Patriots and Revolutionaries 1776-1871*

WAKE UP TO WOKE

It's Time, Australia

Dr Kevin Donnelly AM

Foreword by Senator Jacinta Nampijinpa Price

Published by Impetus Consultants Pty Ltd

Title: Wake Up To Woke: It's Time, Australia

Author: Donnelly, Kevin

ISBN: 978-0-646-89256-6 (print)

Subjects: SOCIAL SCIENCE / Anthropology / Cultural & Social
              POLITICAL SCIENCE / Commentary & Opinion

Book design and layout by Eilidh Direen

Contents

Foreword...9

Introduction..14

The Indigenous Voice to Parliament and Why It Deserved to Fail.....22

Voice failure 'a magnificent result'..23
A true cultural turning point...25
One person, one vote: Australia must say NO to race-based privilege...28
Senator is right to see colonialism as positive.........................31
We should all be proud to be called Australian.........................33
Constitutional change will only serve to divide us all................36
Make no mistake, it really is this simple................................39
Colonial thieves..41
First Fleet did not commit original sin...................................44
Dismissing the details cheapens Voice debate.........................46
Loudest voices often have nothing nice to say.........................49

The Battle of Ideas and the Origins of Woke Ideology...............52

Australia Day-hating Albo not one of us..................................53
Misinformation bill is an attack on freedom rights...................55
Del Noce and eroticism...58
Repressive tolerance: Enforcing mind control and group think...........61
Time for conservatives to call out cancel culture.....................67
Getting to the truth of the transgender theory debate................70
Culture, not science or scepticism, will fulfil us.....................72
Young, free and stronger no more...75
God reigns despite the darkness...78
Oppression of our own big brother..80
Dissident plumbed the future...83
Kooyong and Wentworth: the nowhere lands.............................86
Wokeism: the next big religion...89
Trust me I'm a tree...91
The shame of being white...94
Fundamental flaws in gender theory..96
The moral void at the heart of cancel culture...........................98

Australia's Woke Education System, Dumber and Dumber.......102

Time to take action to empower schools....................................103
Schools for fools: educational corruption.................................105

The Politics of Envy..108
Education destroyed by self-serving educrats.............................111
Curriculums must ward off woke ideology...................................114
Much still to be done to sort out this mess..................................117
There is a right time and place for sex education.......................119
Our schools are failing: this is why..122
Teacher training not the only answer for better outcomes........131
Gender ideology is front and centre in our schools...................133
Enduring truths and neglected lessons..136
Chalk and Cheese: Education Then and Now...............................139
Background no reason for failing standards.................................141
We need to restore the sense of optimism in our kids..............144
Religious freedom is so important for schools............................147
Religious schools have the right to discriminate........................149
The lesson some find difficult to absorb......................................152
Give parents and students choice, not tired mantras.................154
Loss of respect leaves education pointless..................................157
Australia's dumbed down schools are going nowhere...............160
Growing desire for a classical education.....................................162
The barbarians are inside the gates..165

The Road Ahead – In Darkness there is Light............................170

Christianity cornerstone of Western civilisation.........................171
Conservatism in a modern world?...173
The importance of a classical education.......................................176
Looking backwards leads us forwards..180
A light to all the world..182
In times of darkness there is always light....................................184
Woke world is wobbling..187
Let's fight for rational thought and common sense.....................190
Fashionable 'no' but religion is not dead yet...............................192
Great minds agree: preserve the tried, tested and true.............195
The spirit of conservative vision...198

Conclusion..201

Foreword

Senator Jacinta Nampijinpa Price, Senator for the Northern Territory and Shadow Minister for Indigenous Australians.

Every story needs context. In 2017, an exclusive group of activists, academics and so-called "Indigenous Leaders" descended on Uluru in Australia's Northern Territory, to sign what was known as "The Uluru Statement from the Heart."

That Statement, signed by just 250 people – who were invited, not elected – had three demands in it. The first was Voice, the second was Treaty, and the third, Truth. These so-called "leaders" then claimed that this statement was delivered on behalf of all Aboriginal and Torres Strait Islander people in Australia.

After winning the 2022 election, then Prime Minister-Elect Anthony Albanese used the first line of his first speech to acknowledge the traditional owners of the land and commit himself and his Labor party to implementing the Uluru Statement "in full." "Voice, Treaty, Truth" became a sort of battle-cry for the activist class. The Prime Minister even had a shirt made to wear the slogan emblazoned across his chest.

In 2017, I was working as the Indigenous program director at the Centre for Independent Studies and as a councillor on Alice Springs Town Council. Back then, the focus for my husband Colin and I, was raising our four boys in the remote town, and I had put my hand up for the local council because I thought I could help affect change in my community.

As the daughter of a Warlpiri Aboriginal woman from the remote NT town of Yuendumu, and a white-Australian father from Newcastle in New South Wales, I understood two very different cultures intricately, and had spent my entire adult life working to create understanding between Indigenous and non-Indigenous Australia.

It was in 2017 that I waded into the national conversation, with a Facebook post that went viral with my thoughts on our National Day.

Australia Day marks the anniversary of Arthur Phillip's arrival in Sydney Cove and, as such, has been used as a point of contention by Aboriginal activists and their Woke allies who want to change the date or abolish the day altogether.

I argued that while it is important to learn the truth about our history, to acknowledge the good and the bad and learn from both, changing the date or abolishing the celebration, will do nothing to change the past.

And so, I asked then the same questions I ask now. Why aren't the people concerned with the date of Australia Day as concerned about the Aboriginal people affected by domestic violence, alcohol, and drug abuse? Why aren't the marches for murdered Aboriginal women as big as the anti-Australia Day marches that occur each year?

The answer to these questions is obvious, it is because the left's real agenda has nothing to do with helping the vulnerable and marginalised in our community.

The Uluru Statement called for Voice, Treaty and Truth, through "substantive constitutional change and structural reform," but throughout the Voice referendum campaign, we saw the real agenda of the left.

They pitched the Voice as an invitation, a "modest request" from Indigenous Australia. Despite polling to suggest otherwise, the Prime Minister and advocates of the 'Yes' side repeatedly claimed that 80% of Indigenous Australians supported the Voice. The 80% figure was proven to be a lie on referendum day, yet the claim, I believe, highlights a key tactic of the left: using the most marginalised and most vulnerable in our communities to achieve their real agenda.

Some of those who advocated the strongest for the Voice believe Australia to be a horrible and racist country, some have links to Marxism – one even paid respects to "the elders of the communist party" – and some want to "change the system" and "tear down" institutions.

The end goal of this activism was not a simple "advisory body" as they falsely claimed it would be, the goal was not improving the lives of Aboriginal and Torres Strait Islanders, nor was it to improve Indigenous disadvantage, indeed, many of these people would find themselves out of a job if these goals were ever achieved.

The real agenda of the left was a radical change to the Australian constitution. A fundamental altering of our governing document with a view to even more radical and fundamental changes to our country and society. Advocates were only too happy to use the most marginalised Aboriginal and Torres Strait Islander Australians in pursuit of their goals.

There are three ways we can know that this was the case. Firstly, because of the approach they took towards addressing Aboriginal and Torres Strait Islander disadvantage; an approach straight out of the leftist playbook. Secondly, through the exclusivity of the consultation process they used in the creation of the proposal. And lastly, the way in which real solutions were overlooked.

The left took a collectivist approach to link every Australian of Aboriginal and Torres Strait Islander descent into a single victim group with no regard for our differences. They drew no distinction between the well off and the ever-increasing Indigenous middle class of the cities and urban areas, and the poorest, most marginalised in our country who live in rural and remote Australia. Voice advocates refused to consider alternative approaches, they overlooked solutions that we have seen work in parts of Australia and instead claimed that the Voice was the last hope.

While the left's use of marginalised and vulnerable peoples is far from new and by no means unique to Australia, it certainly hits that bit harder when it is your own culture, your own heritage, your own country that they're using to do it.

I have seen up close the real problems being faced by the 'forgotten' Australians, the people living out of sight and out of mind in the most remote parts of the country. Those people who don't have easy access to clean water or fresh food, who don't have access to education, who get medical attention once a week when a doctor flies in, or whose towns don't have emergency services on standby. Many members of my extended family face these problems. They are being overlooked, or worse, used as a political tool.

The Yes campaign's story was, in fact, a negative one. It was a message of emotional blackmail, of gaslighting and guilt, and while it led many Australians to genuinely believe that the Voice was the last hope, that without this change the situations of those who most need our help will not improve, it was ultimately a story of blame.

The key claim in their story was that decades of Indigenous-specific policy and untold billions of dollars had – apparently – not delivered any improvement. They said Australians hadn't been listening to Indigenous needs, that concerns over this proposal were "base racism." They blamed everyday Australians for political failures while simultaneously patronising and removing the agency of many Indigenous Australians.

Australia can be a land of contradictions, and just like the land, Australians themselves are no different. We value both our individuality and our classless society that treats us all the same. Aussies value hard work and humility. Few like to accept a hand up, but most are quick to roll up their sleeves and help a mate. None of us want to see Aussies left behind, ostracized, or forgotten.

That is the story the No side told Australia.

A story of what this country has to offer all Australians, no matter the circumstances they find themselves in. We told the story of an Australia that is better as one together, not two divided.

That was my story, my husband's story, our family's story – our country's story – and it's a true story.

Our campaign name was "Fair Australia," because that is the outcome we wanted. An Australia that remained fair for every individual, where we are each equal before the law, where it doesn't matter if you've been on the land for 60,000 years of have been a citizen for 60 seconds, you will be treated the same.

The slogan on our t-shirts, posters and advertising told that story in seven words: Vote No to the Voice of Division. I believe that it was the unifying story that Australians responded to, and that a simple and true story of unity will guide us as we make our way forward as a country.

The Australian Left has demonstrated to us that grouping Australians and making assumptions about them, blaming them and using guilt politics doesn't work. That trying to give one group of people an extra say, a right not given to others, doesn't pass the pub test. What does work is showing people that they have something to offer that no one else does, and that we can all help each other when we willingly come together.

That story, a story built on the importance of the individual and their contribution to a something bigger than themselves, is the better story.

Introduction

Illustrated by the 2023 Yes campaign for the Indigenous Voice to the commonwealth parliament, it's obvious political correctness (rebadged as Woke) now infects Australian society to such a degree it determines how we use language, how public policies are debated and how the nation defines itself and how governments legislate and act.

Instead of being reasonable and modest as argued by Prime Minister Albanese, the 'Uluru Statement from the Heart' embraces a radical narrative underpinned by post-colonial identity politics and victimhood. The assumption is Australian society is inherently racist and guilty of white supremacism, the arrival of the First Fleet was an invasion and there is nothing beneficial or worthwhile about European settlement and colonisation.

Instead of reasoned debate, it's also true Yes supporters stooped to personal abuse. During the campaign Senator Jacinta Nampijinpa Price was described by Noel Pearson as being caught in a "celebrity redneck vortex", the Liberal Party condemned by the Greens' Leader Adam Bandt as a "small racist rump sliding into irrelevance", and Ray Martin described those responsible for the slogan 'if you don't know, vote no' as "dinosaurs and dickheads".

Such is the power of Woke ideology even after 60% of Australians said no to the Voice, Yes activists refused to accept the democratic result. An unsigned statement written by indigenous leaders argues "deliberate disinformation and misinformation was unprecedented, and it proliferated, unchecked, on social media, repeated in mainstream media and unleashed a tsunami of racism against our people".

Phillip Adams, with a thumb nail dipped in bile argues, the no result is "a dark victory for bigotry and wilful ignorance". Adams' refusal to accept the majority decision reminds one of Bertolt Brecht's comment about the East German communist government, after losing an election, arguing it's time to "dissolve the people and elect another".

It's important to realise there is nothing new or unique about the Yes campaign's adoption of Woke ideology and language. I first warned about the dangers of the cultural-left's political correctness movement over 30 years ago in a newspaper article published in 1993 defending the National Party Leader Tim Fischer.

Echoing recent debates surrounding the Indigenous Voice to parliament Fisher's crime was to argue the Aboriginal community benefitted from the generosity of the Australian taxpayer and that the Canberra based bureaucracy, the Aboriginal and Torres Strait Islander Commission (ATSIC), was inefficient and corrupt.

In the article I defined political correctness as "the way in which the moral guardians of the left attack and censor those who dare to criticise any of the movements championed by progressives over the last 20 years. Women's rights, the environment, the gay-lesbian movement and multiculturalism have all become sacrosanct".

At the same time the American academic Dinesh D'Souza in *Illiberal Education* argued political correctness was infiltrating universities and colleges promoting a range of cultural-left ideologies including "black consciousness and black power, feminism, homosexual rights, and, to a lesser degree, pacifism, environmentalism, and so on".

In another newspaper article titled 'Purely PC madness' and published in 1995 I cited the example of the children's story *The Three Little Pigs* as yet another example proving how political correctness was infiltrating society. In a paper presented to the NSW Geography syllabus committee the story was condemned for promoting a Eurocentric, capitalist mindset.

The author argued, "The story assumes a society with private property and individualised labour. It applauds discipline and hard work and solid stone and brick houses of Europe. It places non-material cultural pursuits second to material and its primary motivation comes from fear of nature, or wilderness, in the form of a wolf".

Since the early to mid 1990s political correctness has morphed into a highly infectious and dangerous form of indoctrination and mind control permeating every aspect of Western societies, including Australia. Society is now one where cultural-left thought police monitor the language we use, control how people think and interact, what happens in schools and universities and how government's determine economic, political and social policies.

Breastfeeding is now known as chest feeding, pronouns like he and she have disappeared to be replaced by they or zie, father's day becomes person's day and Qantas tells its staff, instead of husband and wife, to use the labels spouse and partner.

The school curriculum has especially been targeted by the cultural-left to enforce its radical ideology on unsuspecting and innocent students. Instead of the curriculum being balanced and impartial teachers are told to indoctrinate students on issues like climate change, Aboriginal and Torres Strait Islander history and culture and gender and sexuality.

In resources associated with the neo-Marxist inspired Safe Schools gender fluidity program children are taught boys can be girls and girls can be boys and Australian society is guilty of heteronormativity, transphobia and for enforcing a binary definition of gender and sexuality.

One of the co-designers, Roz Ward argues "Marxism offers both the hope and the strategy needed to create a world where human sexuality, gender and how we relate to our bodies can blossom in extraordinary, new and amazing ways that we can only try to imagine today". So much for education being impartial and objective.

Universities, instead of being committed to a liberal view of education based on wisdom, beauty and truth teach students Western civilisation is exploitive and guilty of white supremacism, that knowledge is a social construct imposed by a capitalist society and their duty is to act as cultural warriors dedicated to overthrowing the status quo.

Academics, like Peter Ridd from James Cook University, who fail to conform are cancelled and others, like the University of Melbourne's feminist academic Holly Lawford-Smith, are vilified and harassed for refusing to comply with the prevailing cultural-left ideology regarding sexuality and gender.

Such is the dominance of Wokeness even guilt by association is enough to have one cancelled. A day after being appointed as the chief executive of the Essendon AFL club Andrew Thorburn was pressured to resign after being condemned as homophobic because he belonged to an orthodox Christian church.

Climate alarmism is yet another example of how irrational and dangerous progressive ideology has become and how powerful it is in determining government policy. Even though Australia's contribution to global emissions is negligible at approximately 1.3% governments have embarked on a quixotic course of action guaranteed to cost billions of dollars, raise the cost of living and vandalise coastal and farming areas.

Ignored is the reality Australia has vast reserves of coal and gas that can be used to drive electric generators and, compared to costly and unreliable solar panels and wind turbines, can operate in all weather conditions, day and night. While nuclear power is increasingly popular overseas, Woke Labor governments continue to denounce what is a readily available, cost effective and safe source of generating power.

Wokeness is now so prevalent adherents no longer disguise their extreme agenda. In Victoria ex-premier Daniel Andrews (aka dictator Dan), when responding to the Covid-19 virus, imposed draconian laws locking down the state, cancelled essential freedoms and liberties, imprisoned people in their homes and employed police tactics reminiscent of communist Russia or China.

In kindergarten and primary schools children are taught they have the freedom to self-identify anywhere on the LGBTIQA+ gender and sexuality spectrum. Young boys are taught men are inherently violent as a result of toxic masculinity and Australian society is inherently misogynist.

Corporations, banks and businesses like Qantas contribute millions of dollars to politically correct causes like the Indigenous Voice even though their primary aim is to make a profit and ensure customers are properly served. Sporting clubs like the AFL demonstrate their progressive credentials by mandating gay pride and indigenous matches and holding Welcome to Country ceremonies on a regular basis.

Such corporations and businesses, as well as government departments, also celebrate gender fluidity events like the IDAHOBIT day and fund programs to ensure positive discrimination for so-called victim groups and to highlight their commitment to cultural-left causes.

The arts, drama and comedy industry, instead of holding a critical and insightful mirror to society and human nature, has also fallen victim to cultural-left mind control and group think. The Melbourne Comedy Festival no longer has the Barry Humphries Award as the comedian and satirist committed a heinous thought crime by questioning whether a man could even truly be a woman.

Another comedian, Kate Hanley Corley, also suffered at the hands of the Melbourne Fringe Festival's thought police by committing the crime of yellowface – in her case playing the role of the Aussie Geisha even though Kate is of European descent.

In an act confusing art with communist inspired agitprop actors and actresses across Australia, after the terrorist organisation Hamas butchered, raped and abducted hundreds of innocent Israelis citizens on October 7th, 2023, displayed their Woke bias and ignorance by wearing Palestinian scarves.

Such is the destructive impact of political correctness that Australia's pre-eminent poet Les Murray condemns it on the basis it relies "on sneers and marginalising its opponents rather than engaging them in spirited argument".

Even more damaging than cultural-left ideology enforcing language control and group think is the fact its origins and rationale are underpinned by a sterile, oppressive Marxist view of society drawing on Lenin's belief "Morality is whatever brings about the success of the proletarian revolution". While justified in terms of promoting equality and liberty for all, history tells us every attempt to bring about a socialist utopia has led to the starvation, imprisonment, suffering and the death of millions.

While not as physically destructive, Woke ideology also represents a threat to Western civilisation. Herbert Marcuse's argument denying free speech and cancelling dissidents is permissible and Roz Ward's conviction students must be taught gender fluidity theory both draw on Marxist theory. By enforcing an absolutist secular view of society and how people define themselves, interact and find meaning it's also true Wokeness adopts an impoverished and bleak view of human nature and how best to lead an enriching life and promote human flourishing.

Denying the spiritual and transcendent, as religion is the opium of the masses and art, literature, music and dance are key parts of the ideological state apparatus employed to oppress and subjugate the 'other', leaves nothing of inherent value or worth. As argued by the American academic George Weigel in *The Cube and Cathedral* "the deepest currents of history are spiritual and cultural, rather than political and economic".

Woke ideology has become so prevalent and extreme even those sympathetic to left-of-centre causes are expressing concern. President Obama, when talking to progressively minded college students, warned about not listening to those they might disagree with and failing to entertain ideas they might find uncomfortable.

In an open letter published by *Harper's Magazine* 150 authors, journalists and public figures expressed concerns about those who responded to politically incorrect ideas and beliefs by being equally doctrinaire and closed. The signatories argued, "The democratic inclusion we want can be achieved only if we speak out against the intolerant climate that has set in on all sides".

A more striking example of those normally considered progressive and left-of-centre criticising Woke ideology are the Australian lesbian campaigners denied the right to exclude transwomen from their forums and meetings.

Cultures evolve and change, and societies rarely remain static. It is also true culture is upstream of politics. The time Robert Menzies was Prime Minister from 1949-1966 was a conservative one characterised by love of country, a commitment to the nuclear family and the belief private enterprise and individual effort were preferable to government intervention and the nanny state.

Gough Whitlam's time was characterised by the 'It's Time' slogan and the promotion of progressive, left-of-centre causes including no-fault divorce, free tertiary education and establishing Medibank. This was also a time of the birth control pill and the counter-culture movement promoting gay/lesbian rights and feminism.

While Wokeness has become more influential and all pervasive since the early 1990s, the resounding No vote to the Indigenous Voice proves the tide is shifting and sanity and common sense might yet prevail. Anecdotal evidence suggests politically correct activists have over played their hand and more and more Australians are saying no to cultural-left indoctrination. Enough is enough.

The argument the nation's origins and subsequent history are riven with white supremacism and colonial exploitation, that society is structurally racist and gender and sexually are social constructs and not God given and biologically determined are now facing a counter-movement.

An ABC Australia Talks National Survey found 68% of respondents believed "political correctness had gone too far". A second survey caried out in 2022 on behalf of the ACU's PM Glynn Institute found 66% of those surveyed believed political correctness was limiting free speech.

The Modern Australian Manners Report by the Australian Seniors Insurance Agency concluded 87.9% of those over 50 believed political correctness was having an adverse impact on society.

An education forum held in Adelaide organised by the 4thekids.com.au movement attracted an audience of about 300 concerned parents and teachers worried about falling standards and their children being indoctrinated with radical sexuality and gender ideology. In a second public forum involving the Victorian member of parliament Moira Deeming and held in Melbourne's western suburbs over 400 attended defending freedom of assembly and freedom of speech.

While only in its infancy it is also true more and more parents and teachers are either home schooling their children or establishing their own schools dedicated to a classical, liberal/ arts education committed to a rigorous curriculum based on Matthew Arnold's concept of "the best that has been thought and said".

Overseas the election of Ron DeSantis in Florida and Glen Youngkin in Virginia is evidence cultural-left ideology is no longer as powerful as it has been as citizens mobilise to defend sanity and reason. The 2023 London Alliance for Responsible Citizenship Forum, attended by over 1000 conservative politicians, academics and cultural-critics, also suggests the tide is turning against cultural-left, nihilistic ideology.

The Indigenous Voice to Parliament and Why It Deserved to Fail

Voice failure 'a magnificent result'

Politicam, 21 October 2023

The resounding 60/40 defeat of Prime Minister Albanese's Indigenous Voice to Parliament is a magnificent result proving how common sense and sanity can overcome Woke ideology intent on dividing the country.

The referendum result also proves how politically inept the Labor Prime Minister is in failing to seek consensus with the Liberal/National opposition and believing he could champion an elitist cause while so many Australians are suffering financial deprivation caused by the government's economic and climate alarmist policies.

The Leader of the Opposition Peter Dutton, on the other hand, demonstrated political insight and acumen by arguing the No case and ensuring the shadow cabinet, despite faux liberals like Simon Birmingham missing in action, followed his example.

Appointing Senator Jacinta Nampijinpa Price, a persuasive and articulate Aboriginal woman with lived experience of remote indigenous communities as shadow Minister for Indigenous Affairs, proved a master stroke.

No amount of misinformation spread by the Labor government and blacktivists about the radical change to the constitution being modest and inconsequential could hide the fact the Voice sought to divide the country based on race.

Privileging one group of Australians based on the fact they were here first makes no sense in a land of immigrants where what counts, instead of ancestry and the colour of your skin, is a person's willingness to work hard, support the common good and be a productive citizen.

There's no doubt, the majority of Australians are fed up with cultural-left ideologues pushing Aboriginal victimhood and identity politics represented by the incessant welcome to country ceremony that treats 96.4% of non-indigenous Australians as strangers in their own land.

Parents and grandparents are also fed up with the school curriculum teaching students to feel guilty by presenting a black armband view of history where Australian society is structurally racist and Western civilisation is characterised by white supremacy.

The reality is the arrival of the First Fleet was never an invasion and, as argued by Senator Price, the overall impact of European settlement has been beneficial. The majority of Aborigines have assimilated and all are equal before the law, have the right to vote and stand for parliament and to be productive citizens.

Instead of talking down the country and its history, as argued by the British conservative author Roger Scruton, while the inner city and Canberra based elites indulge in cultural self-flagellation, the majority of citizens value and appreciate their country and what it has to offer.

Based on Britain's vote to leave the European Union and regain sovereignty Scruton also makes the point while intellectual elites push self-hatred and self-doubt the majority of people are conservative in nature seeking a sense of pride and ownership in the places where they live.

The fact wealthy, privileged inner city electorates and the Australian Capital Territory populated by public servants and over paid bureaucrats were the only areas voting Yes to the referendum proves how correct Scruton is.

The overwhelming majority of Australians in outer metropolitan and rural electorates agreed with Dutton and not Albanese. Even more disturbing for Albanese, similar to the Brexit debate where working class voters deserted the Labour Party, is the next commonwealth election cannot be taken for granted.

As well as being politically inept and pushing a centre-left cause the majority of voters see as irrelevant the Yes campaigners stymied their cause by resorting to personal abuse and vitriol instead of reasoned and rational debate.

Noel Pearson attacking Senator Price as being caught in "a celebrity redneck vortex", the Greens' Leader Adam Bandt describing the Liberal Party as a "small racist rump sliding into irrelevance", and Ray Martin arguing the 'slogan 'if you don't know, vote no' appeals to "dinosaurs and dickheads" caused more harm than good.

What's next? The first thing those leading the Yes campaign, including Albanese, need to realise is the majority of Australians have voted No and it is time for consensus and working together to address indigenous disadvantage.

Marcia Langton arguing "It will be at least two generations before Australians are capable of putting their colonial hatreds behind them and acknowledging that we exist" achieves nothing constructive.

It's also vital, based on the concept of subsidiarity, Aboriginal communities are empowered at the local level and given the expertise, resources and support to take ownership of their own destiny.

The time of Canberra based, self-serving bureaucratic organisations far removed from the harsh realities of isolated communities has passed. Instead of acting unilaterally, it's also time for the Labor government to forsake political point scoring and work with Peter Dutton and the opposition to try and ameliorate what is in many ways an intractable problem.

A true cultural turning point

Spectator Flat White, 20 October 2023

In the week before the Voice referendum the esteemed commentator for the Australian newspaper Paul Kelly argued if the No vote prevailed it would be wrong to see the result as a significant turning point in the battle of ideas. Kelly writes:

If the 'No' vote prevails Dutton must beware an emotional resurgence of populist conservatism and far-right elements driven by the false notion the 'No' vote constitutes a cultural and ideological turning point.

I beg to differ. Putting aside the emotive and misleading phrase "beware an emotional resurgence of populist conservatism and far-right elements", Kelly's argument the referendum's defeat cannot be seen as a significant turning point in the culture wars is inherently flawed.

As argued by the American commentator Andrew Breitbart, culture is upstream of politics. Politicians do not exist in a vacuum and history tells us politicians, whether they know it or not, are influenced and guided by larger cultural and ideological forces.

The Labor Party's slogan 'It's Time' was so successful because it encapsulated the cultural climate of the late 1960s and early 1970s, a time of Woodstock, Vietnam moratoriums, sit-ins, the birth control pill and the age of Aquarius. This was a time of forward-looking progressivism and breaking with the past.

John Howard's argument "we will decide who comes to this country" was instrumental in his victory in the 2001 federal election as a significant number of Australians felt anxious about the uncontrolled arrival of boat people at the nation's borders.

One reason Donald Trump became President was because he energised the great mass of what Hilary Clinton described as the deplorables with the slogan 'Make America Great Again'. It was a slogan that reflected the fear and anger of those less privileged Americans fed up with educated, wealthy, East Coast elites controlling the nation's destiny.

Post-referendum analysis concludes one of the principal reasons the No campaign achieved such a significant victory was because its slogan 'Say No To The Voice Of Division' resonated with voters. Voters prefer national unity where all are treated equally instead of creating two nations based on ancestry and race.

Associated with the call for national unity was the opposition leader Peter Dutton's argument allowing the referendum to succeed would result in yet another Canberra-based elitist bureaucracy.

By saying no to dividing the country into two classes of citizens, with only one with a direct line to government and the executive, and no to creating yet another elitist bureaucracy the No campaign tapped into key narratives associated with the culture wars.

The culture wars refers to the battle of ideas ongoing since the establishment of the Frankfurt School in Germany in the early 1920s by a group of communist academics convinced the best way forward was to take control of key institutions including schools and universities.

The 'Uluru Statement from the Heart', instead of being modest as argued by Albanese, champions neo-Marxist-inspired post-colonial and critical race theories. Western societies like Australia are condemned as structurally racist and non-Indigenous Australians are forever guilty of past, present and future crimes as a result of white supremacy.

Instead of controlling their own lives and being responsible for their actions Aboriginals who succumb to alcoholism, instigate domestic violence, or commit rape are excused on the basis they suffer inter-generational trauma and lateral violence caused by white supremacism.

In opposition to cultural Marxism is what Roger Scruton describes as a "post-war conservative movement" associated with Russell Kirk's book *The Conservative Mind* and William Buckley's journal *National Review*. Central to this movement is a commitment to continuity as well as change and the traditions and institutions associated with Western civilisation that have stood the test of time.

When explaining the unexpected result of the Brexit referendum, where voters decided to withdraw the United

Kingdom from the European Union, Scruton refers to the inherently conservative nature of the British people and their love of country and commitment to family and their local communities.

In opposition to citizens who identify with what is local and feel national pride are what Scruton describes as the intellectual elites who view patriotism as racist, xenophobic, and imperialistic. Similar to journalists arguing No voters are ignorant and easily duped, such elites have a condescending view of any who fail to conform to their Woke ideology.

Yes campaigners championed a black armband view of history where the arrival of the First Fleet was presented as an invasion leading to genocide and argued No voters were racist and ignorant, so it should not surprise so many millions in the outer suburbs and country Australia voted no.

The fact highly educated elites living in the inner city Teal electorates supported the Voice and wealthy corporates from the top end of town including Qantas, BHP, Western Mining, Wesfarmers, and Westpac gave millions to the Yes campaign proves Scruton correct.

Western societies like Australia are divided between wealthy, privileged, cosmopolitan elites and the majority of less affluent, more conservative citizens in the outer suburbs and country Australia who are concerned with immediate practical issues like the cost of living, finding somewhere to live and raising a family in what are difficult and stressful times.

One person, one vote: Australia must say NO to race-based privilege

Spectator Flat White, 13 October 2023

Unlike totalitarian regimes, liberal western democracies like Australia are based on the fundamental principle of one person, one vote. To be legitimate it is essential all citizens are treated equally in their ability to elect and influence the government of the day. To give one group of citizens the unique privilege of having a direct line to parliament and executive government breaches such a principle.

The argument the Indigenous Voice will not have the power to influence government ignores the reality a Labor government will always acquiesce given it relies on the Woke Teals and Greens to pass legislation through the parliament. As admitted by Prime Minister Albanese, it would take a strong government to deny what the Voice demands.

Even worse, if the Yes campaign succeeds there will be no limit on what the Indigenous Voice is able to achieve when it comes to affecting government policy. The Uluru statement argues Indigenous Australians must have "the right to be consulted on legislation and policy that affect Aboriginal and Torres Strait Islander people".

The danger, as Indigenous Australians are Australian citizens, is that it's likely an activist High Court would define the right to be consulted as including any proposed legislation affecting Australian citizens – a category that includes Indigenous Australians.

Crucial to our way of government, one ensuring liberties and freedoms are maintained and governments held to account, is government decisions are open and transparent and voters are critically informed and knowledgeable.

Another reason to vote No is the PM has refused to detail the powers of the Voice including how it will be elected and what checks and balances there will be to ensure it's not an elite, self-serving body mired by corruption like the previous Aboriginal body ATSIC.

The fact the PM remains silent is even more disturbing as the Uluru statement is based on the mistaken premise the arrival of the First Fleet in 1788 was an invasion and the only way forward is for Australia to be divided into two nations – one Aboriginal and one non-Aboriginal.

Instead of being a modest change what the Uluru statement wants is the ability for the Voice to make "agreements at the highest level" where the "Australian government allows First

Nations to express our sovereignty – sovereignty that we know comes from The Law".

Based on what is happening in Canada and New Zealand, where Indigenous rights prevail, if the Voice campaign succeeds there is no doubt Aboriginal activists will demand even more rights based on the concept of Makarrata.

The Uluru statement defines Makarrata as "another word for Treaty or agreement-making". A Treaty, if legislated, that would enable Indigenous Australians to "reclaim control and make practical changes over the things that matter in their daily lives".

Make no mistake, central to the Voice is the radical proposal to cede sovereignty to 3.6% of the population who already own approximately 50% of the land and already receive over $30 billion annually in government support.

While there are substantial reasons why it's OK to vote No, the reality is those campaigning for the Voice to parliament are their own worst enemies. Instead of arguing in a rational and convincing way Yes activists rely on abuse and emotional blackmail.

The columnist Troy Bramston argues, "The No camp is led by populist reactionary conservatives, many of whom have been propagating lies and misinformation about the voice, and some have peddled unadulterated racism".

Geoffrey Robertson's argument the success of the No vote will be seen internationally as "the vote of an ignorant and racist populace", instead of helping the Yes campaign, achieves the opposite.

Evidence proving why such emotive and abusive arguments are wrong include the Mabo High Court decision ceding Aboriginal land rights and the fact there are 11 Indigenous commonwealth members of parliament freely elected based on their character and not the colour of their skin.

There is also evidence, after years of being treated as strangers in their own land and being told every succeeding generation of non-Indigenous Australians will be guilty of the sins of the past, enough is enough. As argued by Senator Price, the time of Woke ideology characterising Indigenous Australians as perennial victims and Australian society as guilty of white supremacism has long since passed.

Senator is right to see colonialism as positive

Daily Telegraph, 3 October 2023

It's understandable why the progressive activists campaigning Yes for the Indigenous Voice to parliament are suffering apoplexy in response to Senator Jacinta Nampijinpa Price's argument the arrival of European settlement, after all, was not such a bad thing.

When asked about the impact of colonialism on Aborigines Price answered, "A positive impact? Absolutely. I mean, now we've got running water, we've got readily available food. I mean everything my grandfather had when he was growing up, because he first saw whitefellas in his early adolescence, we now have".

Price also argues, contrary to the belief Aborigines are eternal victims of white supremacism, it's wrong to characterise indigenous people as powerless and always oppressed and disadvantaged.

In her National Press Club speech Price states, "If we keep telling Aboriginal people that they are victims, well, we are effectively removing their agency… That is the worst possible thing you can do to any human being – to tell them they are a victim without agency and that's what I refuse to do".

While what Price argues is common sense and reasonable to most Australians to the elites campaigning Yes to the referendum Price is guilty of the unforgivable sin of committing thought crime by being politically incorrect.

By opposing the cultural-left's narrative pushing victim hood and identity politics Price has revealed how flawed, counter-productive and self-defeating the ideology underpinning the campaign for the Yes case is.

Central to the Yes case are the concepts of inter-generational trauma and lateral violence. As a result of the First Fleet landing in what is now Sydney 235 years ago past, present and future generations of Aboriginal people are destined to oppression and marginalisation by a supposedly racist society.

Ignored is that Aborigines have equal rights before the law, are entitled to vote and stand for parliament and many have assimilated and lead prosperous lives. Land rights exist as a result of the Mabo High Court decision and Indigenous Australian's receive over $30 billion annually in government support.

Even more self-defeating is the concept of lateral violence. The domestic and sexual violence plus alcoholism prevalent in so many remote indigenous communities, instead of being the result of an individual's actions, is caused by intergenerational trauma.

As argued by the Native Women's Association of Canada, violence and abuse in indigenous communities are caused by "colonisation, oppression, intergenerational trauma and the ongoing experience of racism and discrimination".

Not surprisingly, the Australian Human Rights Commission in its 2011 Social Justice Report written by Mick Gooda, when explaining lateral violence, argues the reason so many isolated indigenous communities are dysfunctional is because Australian society is racist.

The report suggests, such is the power of Australia's white, privileged society, "directing anger and violence toward the colonisers is too risky or fruitless. In this situation we (Indigenous people) are safer and more able to attack those closest to us who do not represent the potent threat of the colonisers".

While there is no doubt the arrival of Europeans in 1788 caused disease, violence and dispossession, as argued by Senator Price, it's self-defeating and counter-productive to condemn succeeding generations of Indigenous Australians to perpetual victimhood.

One of the redeeming qualities of open and free societies like Australia, where liberty and freedom prevail, is individuals are judged by their character and not the colour of their skin and, with initiative, determination and hard work, all have the power to achieve a better life.

It's also wrong to suggest the violence and suffering experienced by Aborigines only started with the arrival of the First Fleet. Aboriginal society before white settlement, instead of being a peaceful utopia, was characterised by inter-tribal warfare, violence against women and uncivilised practices like revenge killing.

Proven by first-hand accounts given by the Royal Marine Watkin Tench who arrived with the First Fleet and William Buckley, an escaped convict who lived with Aborigines on what is now the Bellarine Peninsula, Aboriginal life was especially patriarchal and misogynist.

This dark side of Aboriginal culture has been airbrushed from history and is ignored by the obsequious 'Welcome to Country' ceremony where we are treated as strangers in our own land and made to praise "Elders past and present".

Unlike Julian Lesser who resigned as the Liberal Party's Shadow Minister for Indigenous Australians as he supports the Yes campaign, the current Shadow Minister Senator Jacinta Nampijinpa Price is an Aboriginal woman with first-hand experience of living in an indigenous community.

Her life's story is unique and her speech at the recent National Press Club represents a tipping point in the Voice referendum that will only add to the Yes campaigners' fear the No vote will prevail.

We should all be proud to be called Australian

Daily Telegraph, 8 September 2023

Like the millions of other Australians who can trace their ancestry back to the time before federation in 1901 I'm a proud Australian. The first Donnelly arrived in the colony of New South Wales in 1841 travelling from King's County in Ireland and settling in what is now Wagga Wagga.

The voyage to the fledgling colony was lengthy and arduous on the ship Laurel with one daughter dying before arrival. After disembarking in Sydney John Donnelly, like many before him, decided to try his luck in the bush.

As written in the *Australian Men of Mark*, "He took up land on the Yass river, near Gundaroo, and remained there on his Bywong Station for many years, proving very successful in agricultural and pastoral pursuits".

Donnelly was so successful breeding sheep for wool to be sold in London his property had a forty mile frontage on the Murrumbidgee river and he was able to buy land on which the Sisters of the Presentation of the Blessed Virgin Mary built their convent.

There is nothing unique in Donnelly's story, but ignored by those seeking to paint our past as oppressive and racist is the fact, if not for the ambition, hard work and toil of the early pioneers and settlers, Australia would not be such a prosperous nation.

As detailed in Judith Wright's poem *Bullocky* current generations need to acknowledge those long past who struggled in such an inhospitable outback environment. Wright writes, "O vine, grow close upon the bone and hold it with your rooted hand. The prophet Moses feeds the grape and fruitful is the promised land".

At a time when Senator Lidia Thorpe and the radical indigenous activist Thomas Mayo champion a black armband view of history it's time for native-born Australians to stand proud and celebrate the nation's history.

A nation, for all its faults and sins, that was one of the first to give women the vote and that introduced a conciliation and arbitration system plus the eight-hour day to protect workers' rights and those doing it hard.

Instead of invading the orders given to the colony's first governor were to treat Aborigines with respect and kindness and to peacefully co-exist. Even though a number of convicts were killed Phillip refused to retaliate unless absolutely necessary.

As noted by Tim Flannery in *Watkin Tench 1788*, "Indeed, in all, the Aborigines were able to kill or severely wound seventeen Europeans (including Governor Phillip himself), with no loss to themselves, before a reprisal was ordered".

Forget original sin where blacktivists argue every generation of non-Indigenous Australians is guilty of alleged crimes committed over 235 years ago when the penal colony was established in what is now Sydney.

Also forget the claim, epitomised by the obsequious 'Welcome to Country' celebration where we are treated as strangers trespassing on our own land, that we don't have the right to call Australia home.

To argue any who say No to the Voice being enshrined in the constitution are racist and that the needs of Aborigines and Torres Strait Islanders are ignored is also a myth perpetuated by those committed to identity politics and victimhood.

Indigenous Australians have long since had the right to vote, to be treated equally before the law and every year receive more than $30 billion in government benefits. Indigenous Australians also have land rights and interests in about 50% of Australia's land mass.

While there's no doubt many Indigenous Australians suffer deprivation, ill health and poverty it's also true there are countless others who have assimilated and are leading a prosperous life. Warren Mundine, Senator Jacinta Nampijinpa Price and Anthony Dillion, all Aborigines arguing the No case, illustrate what can be achieved.

Instead of fermenting division by dividing the nation into two types of citizens, those who have a direct line to executive government to influence decision making and the other 96% denied such preferential treatment, it's time to forget past grievances and move on.

Instead of romanticising Aboriginal culture and history before European settlement as an antipodean Garden of Edan and promoting a black armband view of European settlement what is needed is a reality check.

Pre-European Aboriginal culture, like many other less developed cultures, was characterised by violence, ill health and inequality – especially for women. The grievance industry portraying Indigenous Australians as perennial victims is also counterproductive and self-defeating.

As argued by Senator Price, it's time to draw a line in the sand and embrace a future where all Australian citizens, instead of the colour of their skin, are judged according to their character and their willingness to embrace a future united by what we hold in common.

Constitutional change will only serve to divide us all

Daily Telegraph, 13 June 2023

The 'Uluru Statement From the Heart' that calls for "the establishment of the First Nations Voice enshrined in the Constitution" recently celebrated its 6th anniversary and it should be compulsory reading for all citizens eligible to vote in the forthcoming referendum.

Prime Minister Albanese describes the Uluru Statement as a "gracious request" designed to "bring us all closer together as a people reconciled – and to lift our great nation even higher".

In arguing the Uluru Statement unifies the nation the Prime Minister has either not read it, or if he has, is not willing to admit it creates two classes of citizens in perpetuity based on whether they are Indigenous or non-Indigenous.

Unlike the over 96% of Australians who are non-Indigenous those who identify as Aboriginal and Torres Strait Islander will be granted the unique privilege of being able to "make representations to the Parliament and Executive Government of the Commonwealth".

No other citizen has that right enshrined in the constitution and as admitted by Prime Minister Albanese, only a strong government would deny any request made by the Voice, no matter how costly, ineffective or counter-productive.

In addition to creating two classes of citizens and contrary to the Prime Minister's plea to be on the right side of history the Voice also represents an egregious attack on the nation's Westminster inspired parliamentary and legal systems.

Make no mistake, if the referendum is passed the nation will face an irreversible change to the constitution. A constitution that has ensured over 122 years of peace and prosperity and led to Australia attracting millions from around the world seeking a new and better life.

Instead of being a modest change, as Prime Minister Albanese repeatedly argues, the Uluru Statement demands far-reaching "substantive constitutional change and structural reform".

Similar to the independent Senator Lydia Thorpe, who wants to create a nation within a nation, the Uluru Statement also argues Indigenous Australians must control their own destiny and no longer be part of Australia as a unified nation.

The Uluru Statement argues Indigenous Australians define sovereignty as a "spiritual notion" that it "has never been ceded or extinguished" and it "co-exists with the sovereignty of the crown".

Indigenous activists want to create two nations with the so-called First Nations having the unique privilege of having a direct line to executive government. As argued by *The Australian's* Paul Kelly, the real agenda is all about power.

Those arguing both Indigenous and non-Indigenous nations will be treated equally also ignore the past judgments of the High Court where legal activism prevails. The reality, sooner or later, is that the Voice's demands will be given priority. So much for popular sovereignty.

There is no doubt too many Indigenous Australians suffer poverty, domestic violence and sexual abuse but, instead of accepting those responsible must be held to account, the Uluru Statement blames Australian society for being structurally racist.

Drawing on Woke ideology associated with the neo-Marxist inspired Black Lives Matter movement the argument is indigenous deprivation, pain and suffering are caused by lateral violence. Individuals are not responsible for their own actions as white supremacism is always to blame.

The reason there is so much violence caused by Aboriginal youth in Alice Springs and why so many Aboriginal women and young girls face sexual abuse, supposedly, is because of events that happened over 235 years ago when the First Fleet landed and the British flag was raised at Sydney Cove.

Before the British arrived, apparently, there was no inter-tribal warfare or violence and women were never treated unjustly as all lived in a pristine utopia where nature provided all that was necessary and peace and harmony prevailed.

The 'Uluru Statement From the Heart' as well as presenting a black armband and mythical view of Australian history also ignores the reality, compared to the Uyghurs in China, the Christians in the Middle East and the Kurds in Turkey and Iraq, Indigenous Australians already have a voice and are much better off.

Indigenous Australians receive over $30 billion in tax-payer funds annually, according to the National Indigenous Australians Agency have recognised rights in around 50 per cent of Australia's land mass and have the same freedoms and liberties as other Australians.

Add the fact Indigenous Australian's already have a voice represented by the 11 Commonwealth members of parliament and the thousands of indigenous corporations and bodies across the nation it's obvious what is not needed is yet another expensive, Canberra-based bureaucracy.

The preamble to the Australian Constitution, the nation's founding document, includes the words "have agreed to unite in one indissoluble Federal Commonwealth". What the Indigenous Voice seeks to do is to cancel the enduring bond that unites us.

Make no mistake, it really is this simple

Quadrant Online, 12 April 2023

After the personal abuse directed at Julian Leeser, the former shadow attorney-general, it's no wonder he decided to resign from the frontbench, thus giving him the freedom to campaign for a Yes victory in the upcoming referendum. His departure to the backbench is a further consequence of one of the most disappointing strategies employed by Voice supporters — instead of civilised and rational debate when weighing arguments for and against we see a blitz of personal attacks, vitriol and emotive language.

In response to Peter Dutton's decision to argue for the No vote, Noel Pearson described the opposition leader as an "undertaker" responsible for burying the 'Uluru Statement From the Heart'. Especially egregious, given Easter's celebration of Christ's betrayal, crucifixion and resurrection, is Pearson's condemnation of the Liberal Party's decision as a "Judas betrayal".

Prime Minister Anthony Albanese also paints Dutton as an undertaker burying the Uluru statement while citing the decision to oppose the Voice as an example of "taking the low road". Greens leader Adam Bandt also employs emotive language when describing Dutton as an incendiarist seeking to "ignite a culture war".

Over the last two months those in favour of the Voice have cheapened the debate by arguing anyone who votes No is a bad person and, even worse, if the referendum fails Australia will be seen by the rest of the world as racist and guilty of white supremacism.

At a time when emotion and ad hominem attacks are so prevalent, instead of rational, reasoned debate, it should not surprise critics have ignored the reasons why Dutton and many of those in the party room oppose the Voice.

In an email sent to Liberal Party members, after agreeing there should be indigenous recognition in the Constitution, Dutton, in opposition to a Canberra-centric, bureaucratic organisation, argues in favour of "local and regional bodies to provide grassroots advice". Prioritising and empowering those at the local level, in opposition to elitist, centralised bodies far removed from the practicalities experienced by those on the ground, is a central tenet of Liberal Party philosophy.

As argued by F A Hayek in *The Road To Serfdom* while statism embodies centralised control and a top-down model of governance far more efficient and morally superior is subsidiarity where the individuals most affected work together to address common problems and issues.

In acknowledging the importance of conservatism Sir Robert Menzies often spoke of the dangers arising from centre-left parties imposing a collectivist, inflexible and inefficient approach to public policy and governance. Whereas Albanese argues voters should support the Indigenous Voice in order to remain true to the vibe Dutton refers to the need to think carefully about the "unknown consequences" arising from such a significant and fundamental change to the Constitution.

Especially concerning is Part 2 of the proposed change to the constitution that states, "The Aboriginal and Torres Strait Islander Voice may make representations to the Parliament and the Executive Government of the Commonwealth on matters relating to Aboriginal and Torres Strait Islander peoples".

English philosopher Michael Oakeshott in his essay 'On Being Conservative' makes a similar point to Dutton when suggesting, when considering change, "the disruption entailed has always to be set against the benefit anticipated". Dutton argues "The facts matter. The details matter" and, if the referendum is passed, there is every chance the Voice "will subsume parliamentary sovereignty and lead to "intervention by an activist High Court."

One of the cornerstones of Western liberal democracies dating back to *Magna Carta*, the Glorious Revolution and the evolution of universal suffrage is popular sovereignty where all citizens are treated equally and have the right to vote. The right to what the American Declaration of Independence describes as "Life, Liberty and the pursuit of Happiness" is not decided by the colour of one's skin, one's gender or one's position in society.

Giving Indigenous Australians the unique right to affect government policy and actions by allowing them to appeal directly to parliament as well as the executive government creates two classes of citizens where one has more power and special privilege based on the colour of their skin and ancestry.

Oakeshott argues whenever significant change is suggested "the onus of proof, to show that the proposed change may be expected to be on the whole beneficial, rests with the would-be innovator".

In particular, that the intended change "is least likely to be corrupted by undesired and unmanageable consequences". To date, requirements that Albanese and those in favour of the Voice have failed to provide.

Colonial thieves

Spectator Flat White, 17 February 2023

There's no end to the cultural-left pushing Yes to the Indigenous Voice in the nation's classrooms. The left-leaning Australian Education Union fully supports the 'Uluru Statement from the Heart' and argues Truth-Telling should be taught "in schools through and in the curriculum and in the Australian Professional Standards for Teachers".

Schools across Australia are teaching Bruce Pascoe's *Dark Emu* to students; a book criticised by Peter O'Brien as well as Peter Sutton and Keryn Walshe as misleading and inaccurate when depicting Aboriginal history and culture as sophisticated.

In Victoria, the Minister for Education Natalie Hutchins, who subsequently tried to walk back on the comment, states "The voice referendum will be a defining moment in our nation's history" and it should be dealt with in schools as students need to understand "Victoria's journey to the Treaty".

Not surprisingly, a poetry anthology set for Victoria's Year 12 English titled *False Claims Of Colonial Thieves* by Charmaine Papertalk-Green and John Kinsella is yet another disturbing example of the school curriculum being used to indoctrinate vulnerable students regarding Aboriginal exploitation and oppression.

According to the reviewer at the Sydney Arts Guide the poetry anthology is "a pin prickling polemic" where the poems are "Flinty and unflinching" and act like "depth charges of various C-bombs – Colonisation, Capitalism, Culture and Country". The reviewer lauds the two authors for exposing the "genocide, rape and apartheid" inflicted as a result of European settlement.

Bruce Pascoe, the self-styled indigenous person made famous by his assertion Aborigines were highly civilised at the time of the First Fleet, also recommends the anthology. Pascoe writes the poets "take no prisoners" and it is not for the light-hearted as it depicts the "darkness" at the heart of Australia.

The historian Geoffrey Blainey uses the expression the black armband view to describe those guilty of painting the nation's history as violent, oppressive, racist and Eurocentric. Often ignored is that Blainey also condemns the three cheers view.

The Year 12 anthology provides multiple examples of the black armband view. One poem talks about "Past injustices, cultural cruelty, cultural genocide" while another begins with the lines "The state is killing our souls, The State has murdered the people".

A third poem titled 'Always Thieves' argues those who arrived as a result of 1788, including "Colonial officers, convicts, settlers, free man", are all thieves and the injustice and theft continues to this day involving "Mining companies, politicians, governments" with "Dirty hands coated with traces of blood".

A fourth poem called 'Don't mine me' leaves students in no doubt as to who deserves to be condemned when the poets write "Don't mind me Australia… While you are busy… Sticking explosives everywhere… Getting a hard on blowing up land… Pumping chemicals deep into mother… Drip feeding our waters with poison".

Drawing on post-colonial theory and the Black Lives Matter movement where the assumption is societies like Australia are structurally racist the anthology tells students indigenous voices are always silenced when they write "You don't want me to talk about… The concept and construct of whiteness".

It's ironic, at the same time the two poets in the Prologue argue mining companies are guilty of inflicting propaganda on schools about the value and importance of mining they appear unaware they are also guilty of indoctrinating students.

One of the exercises related to the *False Claims of Colonial Thieves* anthology, after adopting the persona of an exploited Aboriginal community, asks students to write to mining companies like BHP telling them to stop exploiting Aboriginal land and destroying the environment.

Even worse, as argued by Mark Lopez in *School Sucks* and who tutors Year 12 students in Victoria, the reality is the poetry anthology is just one of many chosen texts that "are overwhelmingly politically correct and left-wing".

While students across Australia are presented with a jaundiced and one-sided view of indigenous affairs and the impact of European settlement ignored are the facts, compared to the Uyghurs in China and the Kurds in the Middle East, Aborigines have achieved equality and the sins of the past long since been addressed.

Instead of schools presenting students with an objective and impartial account of controversial issues like the Voice to parliament the sad fact is the cultural-left has long succeeded in using the school curriculum to advance its ideology. Worse still, this has happened under both Labor and Liberal/National governments, state and commonwealth.

First Fleet did not commit original sin

Daily Telegraph, 23 January 2023

The announcement by Prime Minister Anthony Albanese to overturn the decision by the Scott Morrison government to punish local councils for refusing to hold citizenship ceremonies on the 26th of January has reignited the debate about the significance of Australia Day.

Indigenous activists condemn the arrival of the First Fleet as an invasion leading to genocide. Stan Grant, who describes himself as a "proud Wiradjuri man", describes the arrival of Europeans as the nation's "original sin". A sin that still exists after hundreds of years and will continue to stain innocent generations for years to come.

In the Australian national curriculum students are told the convict settlement "was viewed by First Nations Australians as an invasion" leading to "dispossession and the loss of lives through frontier conflict, disease and loss of food sources and medicine".

While there is no doubt the establishment of the penal colony and its gradual expansion led to Aborigines suffering dislocation, disease and violence at the same time the reality, compared to Russia's invasion of the Ukraine, is that it's wrong to describe European settlement as an invasion.

The Admiralty's orders to Captain Arthur Phillip stated, "You are to endeavour by every possible means to open an Intercourse with the Natives and to conciliate their affections, enjoining all Our Subjects to live in amity and kindness with them".

The fact Phillip took no reprisal after being speared and convicts were punished when they ignored Phillip's orders to treat any Aborigines encountered with respect also prove how wrong it is to describe the penal colony as an invasion.

As noted by Watkin Tench, one of the marines who arrived with the First Fleet, "all ranks of men have tried to effect it (to coexist peacefully with the Aborigines) by every reasonable effort from which success might have been expected I can testify".

While many denounce Australia Day as Sorry Day and argue there is nothing beneficial or worthwhile about the 26th of January the reality is this was the day Phillip raised the British flag in Sydney Cove proving to the French, who had recently arrived in Botany Bay, this was a British colony.

Unlike the French, who were soon to experience the violence and terror of the 1789 revolution, a colony that inherited a political and legal system drawing on the *Magna Carta* and Blackstone's *Commentaries on the Laws of England* that embodied essential rights and freedoms.

A colony that also drew on Enlightenment values such as liberty, reason and tolerance that help explain why the British were the first to abolish slavery. Such was the strength of the anti-slavery movement Phillip argued in the new colony "there can be no slavery in a free land, and consequently no slaves".

Proven by the arrival of the *King James Bible* and the first church service held on the 3rd of February 1788 by the Reverend Richard Johnson Australia's foundation is also deeply imbued with Christianity.

Central to Jesus' teachings is what St Paul describes as the belief "There is neither Jew nor Greek, there is neither bond nor free, there is neither male nor female: for ye are all one in Christ Jesus".

Concepts like the inherent dignity of the person, the right to freedom and liberty and a commitment to social justice and serving the common good are biblical in origin. While not always followed, over time such Christian teachings have ensured Western societies like Australia are beacons of freedom in an increasingly hostile world.

One of the mantras employed by Aboriginal activists is this is the time for truth telling. The same applies to both sides of the debate. Rather than condemning the arrival of the First Fleet as an invasion leading to genocide it's time to tell the truth.

The evidence proves, notwithstanding the eventual violence, dispossession and disease following the colony's expansion across the Blue Mountains, the original intention was to treat the Aborigines fairly.

It's also true since January 26th 1788 Aborigines have benefited from European settlement proven by the right to vote, to be treated equally before the law and decisions like Mabo guaranteeing land rights. While representing 3.6% of the population it's also true Aborigines receive approximately $30 billion annually in government grants, subsidies and payments.

It should not be ignored before European settlement, instead of being the First Nations, there were hundreds of different Aboriginal tribes and violence and warfare existed as it always has among other cultures and throughout history.

Dismissing the details cheapens voice debate

Daily Telegraph, 18 January 2023

Prime Minister Albanese, in response to the Opposition Leader Peter Dutton's request for details about how the Voice, if enshrined in the constitution, would be implemented tweeted "People are over cheap culture war stunts".

In rejecting Dutton's request by describing it as a culture war stunt the Prime Minister inadvertently reveals what is most disturbing about the Indigenous Voice to parliament and why citizens have every right to be given details about what the Voice entails if the referendum is passed.

Underlying arguments for the Voice is the belief Western societies like Australia are inherently racist and oppressive. The 'Uluru Statement from the Heart' argues indigenous disadvantage is "structural" inevitably leading to the "torment of the powerlessness".

Drawing on politically correct ideology, identity politics and victimhood prevail where white people are bigoted and advantaged and indigenous people abused and ill-treated.

Instead of characterising the culture wars as a stunt the reality is since the Frankfurt School was established in Germany during the late 1920s by a group of Marxist academics the culture wars have dominated the West.

The British politician Michael Gove argues "The thinkers of the Frankfurt School revised Marxism as primarily a cultural rather than an economic movement. In place of anger at traditional capitalism, scorn was directed at the reigning values of the West".

In his book *The Long March* the American academic Roger Kimball also argues academics associated with the Frankfurt School, including Herbert Marcuse, Eric Fromm and Wilhelm Reich, turned their backs on classical Marxism.

Instead of storming the barricades and having a revolution as occurred in communist Russia Kimball writes "utopian efforts to transform society have been channelled into cultural and moral life".

As argued by the Marxist Herbert Marcuse the best way to take control is by "working against established institutions while working within them". Roger Scruton in *Culture Counts* details at some length how pervasive cultural-left ideology now is.

Scruton argues a "culture of repudiation" drawing on neo-Marxist critical theory (a child of the Frankfurt School) dominates the West's universities, schools, the media and public and political discourse.

A rainbow alliance of radical theories including Foucault's argument knowledge is a social construct reinforcing power relations and Edward Said's view Western civilisation is inherently xenophobic and imperialist are now the dominant orthodoxy.

As a result, Scruton warns the belief "rational inquiry leads to objective truth" is replaced by the cultural-left's argument such is the oppressive nature of Enlightenment thinking "Reason, therefore, is a lie, and by exposing the lie we reveal the oppression at the heart of Western culture".

Such has been the success of what the German radical Rudi Dutschke describes as the long march through the institutions cultural-left ideology is now all pervasive. In England, America and Australia statues are destroyed, students taught Western civilisation is inherently oppressive and freedom of speech cancelled by what the American journalist Bari Weiss describes as Orwellian wrong think.

Proven by the success of republican governors such as Ron DeSantis in Florida and Glenn Youngkin in Virginia and the ground swell of community hostility across America to Woke ideology and critical race theory not all is lost.

The movement against politically correct Wokeism is also evident in England where Liz Trust, before she became Prime Minister, argued in favour of "the core principles of freedom, choice, opportunity, and individual humanity and dignity" in opposition to the cultural-left's belief Western societies are always corrupt.

Kemi Badenoch is another English politician willing to engage in the culture wars and defend rational thought, freedom of expression and the need, for all its faults, to acknowledge and respect Western culture.

In opposition to the Black Lives Matter inspired campaign to de-colonise the school curriculum by painting Western culture as racist and guilty of white supremacism, Badenoch argues "schools have statutory duty to remain politically impartial".

The Australian Constitution is one of the bedrocks of the nation's political, legal and economic system that has stood the test of time and ensured Australia is such a liberal, democratic and peaceful nation where freedoms and rights are protected.

To argue indigenous rights must be enshrined in the constitution represents a far reaching and significant change and Peter Dutton, on behalf of the millions of citizens entitled to vote in the forthcoming referendum, has every right to ask for the details about the Voice.

By dismissing Dutton's request as a culture war stunt the Prime Minister cheapens the debate and avoids detailing the impact of what is such a far reaching and consequential change.

Loudest voices often have nothing nice to say

Daily Telegraph, 14 December 2022

Cultural-left activists, when it comes to supporting the Indigenous Voice, are happy to use highly charged, emotional language to shut down debate and cancel any opposition. Instead of rationality and reason prevailing activists employ hyperbole and attack the person.

Instead of having a proper debate those in favour of the Voice argue they are on the right side of history while any who oppose the Voice are destined to be on the wrong side.

The Green Party's Senator Sarah Hanson-Young denounces the National Party's opposition to the Voice as being on the wrong side of history while both the Prime Minister, Anthony Albanese, and Linda Burney, the Minister for Indigenous Australians, describe those in favour as being on the right side of history.

While arguing opponents to the Voice are on the wrong side of history might give those advocating the Voice a warm inner glow of moral superiority as history will prove them right and their opponents wrong, the reality is matters are not that straightforward or simple.

Very few, if any, have a crystal ball allowing them to know the future as what happens is rarely linear and predictable. The poet Wordsworth's exuberant praise in response to the French Revolution failed to predict Madame Guillotine and the reign of terror.

The *Communist Manifesto*'s belief in the historical destiny of the workers' revolution and socialist utopia proved incorrect. The British Prime Minister Neville Chamberlain's boast after meeting Adolf Hitler there would be "peace in our time" was also proven untrue with the passing of time.

Assigning history with some moral purpose where the passage of time will identify those on the right side and those on the wrong side based on contemporary beliefs and values is also tenuous.

As argued by Martin Luther King Jr in his 'Letter from a Birmingham Jail', "Such an attitude stems from a tragic misconception of time, from the strangely irrational notion that there is something in the very flow of time that will inevitably cure all ills. Actually, time itself is neutral; it can be used either destructively or constructively".

Condemning any who doubt or criticise the Voice as being on the wrong side of history is only one example of how the cultural-left shuts down debate and cancels opposition. Other examples include using emotional and exaggerated language and attacking the person instead of the argument.

Noel Pearson, after David Littleproud the leader of the National Party announced the party opposes the Voice, described him as "a man of little pride' and a "kindergarten kid".

In *The Sydney Morning Herald* newspaper Nick Bryant, an academic at the University of Sydney, implies voting against the Voice would demonstrate to those overseas Australia is "a redneck nation" and provide proof "the country is a racial rogue nation".

If the referendum failed Bryant also argues it would leave "an indelible stain" proving the nation "could not break free from its racist past". The prize for the most extreme example of highly emotionally charged language goes to the indigenous academic Marcia Langton in a recent ABC interview.

After condemning the National Party's opposition to the Voice as injecting "misinformation and vitriol into the debate", Langton implies opponents are guilty of causing the debate to "sink into a nasty, highly eugenicist, 19th-century style of debate about the superior race versus the inferior race".

Using emotive and exaggerated language is a poor substitute for logic, rationality and reason when debating significant, complex issues. As the Voice is such an important issue it deserves more than suggesting opponents are rednecks, racists and rogues.

The fact indigenous public figures like Senator Jacinta Nampijinpa Price and the Indigenous leader Warren Mundine put forward a number of reasoned arguments against the Voice proves not all opponents are white bigots.

It's not just debates about the Voice where the cultural-left forsakes balance and reason. Express misgivings about multiculturalism and you are condemned as xenophobic and racist. Suggest it's OK for woman to be feminine and you are sexist and if you argue against gender transitioning you are transphobic.

George Orwell writes "But if thought corrupts language, language can also corrupt thought" and in his dystopian novel *1984* Big Brother and the Party dominate and control citizens by manipulating language. "War is peace, freedom is slavery and ignorance is strength".

Such is the world we now live in where teaching clear thinking has long been abandoned in schools, emotion instead of rationality and reason is all pervasive and where extremists of the left refuse to tolerate and respect any who disagree. Intolerance masquerades as tolerance.

The danger, once reasoned dialogue and debate are no longer possible, is that people resort to vitriol, abuse and, in the end, violence.

The Battle of Ideas and the Origins of Woke Ideology

Australia Day-hating Albo not one of us

Politicam, 26 January 2024

The leader of the opposition Peter Dutton is 100% correct to call on shoppers to boycott Woolworths and Prime Minister Albanese, once again, proves what a tin ear he has when it comes to appreciating the national psyche.

Woolworths cancelling Australia Day merchandise after campaigning for the Yes Voice to parliament last year and printing a Welcome to Country acknowledgement on receipts proves how misguided and out of touch the company is.

More importantly, what the Prime Minister and Woolworths' boss Bradd Banducci fail to understand, proven by what happened to Budd Light in America and the 60/40 No vote to the Voice to parliament, is people are fed up with virtue signalling and cancel culture.

Forget trying to out-woke the woke. The primary aim of businesses, whether Qantas, Woolworths, the big banks or BHP, is to make a profit, provide a good service and ensure shareholders receive a fair return on their investments.

Instead of cancelling the 26th of January history tells us raising the flag at Sydney Cove and toasting the King signify the birth of Australia as one of the world's most successful Western, liberal democracies.

Arriving with the First Fleet was Blackstone's *Commentaries on the Laws of England* that provided a unique concept about ensuring the rule of law and protecting the right to own property, enter contracts and establish a business.

It's no accident one of the first court cases in the fledgling colony involved a married convict couple successfully getting recompense from a captain responsible for losing their belongings on the voyage to Botany Bay.

The fact the *King James Bible* also arrived with the First Fleet also explains why Australia is such a popular and much sought after destination for the millions of immigrants from around the world escaping war, violence, poverty and oppression.

The way blacktivists and Woke warriors trash 26th of January as Australia Day while forcing everyone to celebrate and laud Aboriginal history is a perfect example of what George Orwell describes as Doublethink.

Also known as cognitive dissonance, the process involves holding two conflicting ideas or beliefs at the one time while not realising they contradict one another.

While Yes Voice campaigners like Marcia Langton and Thomas Mayo argue we must acknowledge and respect Aboriginal history when it comes to the nation's history our patrimony is trashed.

Blacktivists argue the arrival of the First Fleet in 1788 signalled an invasion by white supremacists, there is nothing beneficial or worthwhile about European settlement and every citizen not claiming Aboriginal ancestry is guilty of the sins of the past.

Local councils cancelling Australia Day citizenship ceremonies and the national curriculum prioritising Aboriginal history to the detriment of Australia's origins and evolution as a modern, liberal democracy are also guilty of Doublethink.

Instead of romanticising Aboriginal culture and history it's time to reveal the truth. Using the description First Nations to describe the way pre-European Aborigines lived is a myth perpetuated by those fabricating history.

What Europeans discovered on arrival, instead of nations, were hundreds of diverse tribes with different languages, customs and rituals. Proven by accounts given by early explorers and settlers inter-tribal warfare was common where no quarter was given and the vanquished often cannibalised.

Aboriginal culture was also misogynistic as women had few, if any, rights and were often appallingly treated. Watkin Tench, a marine with the First Fleet, writes "But indeed the women are in all respects treated with savage barbarity."

"Condemned not only to carry the children but all other burthens, they meet in return for submission only with blows, kicks and every other mark of brutality. When an Indian (Aboriginal) is provoked by a woman, he either spears her or knocks her down on the spot".

While there's no doubt establishing a convict settlement and the colony expanding across the Blue Mountains caused significant and on-going distress and harm to Aborigines as their land was taken often by violence, it's also true European settlement was beneficial.

Senator Jacinta Nampijinpa Price, when asked about the impact of colonialism, answered "A positive impact? Absolutely. I mean, now we've got running water, we've got readily available food. I mean everything my grandfather had when he was growing up, because he first saw whitefellas in his early adolescence, we now have".

In addition to many Aborigines becoming assimilated into mainstream society, instead of being excluded and treated as outcasts, Indigenous Australians have the same legal rights and protections as non-indigenous Australians including the right to establish businesses.

What companies like Woolworths need to understand is it's only because of the 26th of January they can operate free of corruption and unwarranted government interference and have the freedom to make a profit. To think otherwise is deluded.

Misinformation bill is an attack on freedom rights

Daily Telegraph, 27 October 2023

After losing the Voice referendum because of what supporters claim was deliberate misinformation and lying spread by the No campaign the Labor government is keen to control social media platforms to ensure it dictates the public narrative.

As argued by the political commentator Niki Savva, such was the success of the No's social media strategy in persuading electors to vote no, the Labor Party is worried the same digital strategy will be used at the next federal election to defeat the Albanese government.

One of the basic tenets of Western liberal democracies like Australia is freedom of speech, freedom of conscience and freedom of the press. Especially when it comes to controversial and contentious issues like the Voice it's vital there is robust and rigorous debate.

It's increasingly obvious, under the Albanese Labor government, such freedoms are under attack. The government's plan to legislate to fine digital platforms for publishing what it defines as misinformation and disinformation is the first threat.

If parliament endorses the planned legislation the government will give the Australian Communication and Media Authority, like Orwell's Ministry of Truth in *1984*, the power to penalise digital platforms for spreading what it defines as misinformation and disinformation.

The Minister for Communication Michelle Rowland states, "If platforms fail to act to combat misinformation and disinformation over time, the ACMA would be able to draw on its reserve powers to register enforceable industry codes with significant penalties for non-compliance".

Such is the vague and broad definition of what constitutes fake news the Australian Human Rights Commission argues the proposed legislation represents a clear and present danger to freedom of expression and freedom of conscience.

The commission warns a key problem with the legislation is it fails to achieve the right balance between free and open comment and what will be censored. The danger is simply because an opinion is unpopular or controversial it will be cancelled.

Even more concerning is while the government of the day is exempt from the proposed legislation any comments or arguments posted on digital platforms by the opposition, minor parties or independents are included and liable to be silenced.

In addition to the Human Rights Commission, the Australian Catholic Bishops also express concerns the government's plan to control what digital platforms are able to publish represents a danger to free and open debate.

Given the increasing climate of censoring religious beliefs regarding controversial subjects like gender transitioning and euthanasia the bishops warn "There are people who will sometimes incorrectly claim the teachings of the Church are hateful and harmful" and thus labelled as misinformation and disinformation.

A second threat to freedom of expression, conscience and the press, including digital platforms, is the Albanese government's inquiry into Australia's Human Rights Framework, including the option of legislating a Human Rights Act.

Unlike overseas countries like America, Canada and South Africa that have a bill of rights in their constitution Australia does not have a national charter of human rights, relying instead on the constitution and state, territory and commonwealth legislation and the common law.

Given the prevalence of legal activism and lawfare, where the legal system is used to punish and silence opponents, if a Human Rights Act is legislated the danger is those who espouse beliefs or views in opposition to the prevailing radical zeitgeist will be punished.

While protecting human rights is a good thing recent history shows human rights legislation is weighted against free speech and freedom of conscience. The conservative Christian Lyle Shelton faced court after being accused of vilification for criticizing the library appearance of drag queens on his blog.

Israel Folau was publicly vilified as well as excluded from playing rugby for Australia for posting his anti-gay Christian views on his Twitter (now X) and Instagram accounts. Given the recent decision to stop lesbian groups from excluding transwomen from their forums, it's not just Christians who are at risk.

John Stuart Mill, the author of *On Liberty*, argues "If all mankind minus one, were of one opinion, and only one person were of the contrary opinion, mankind would be no more justified in silencing that one person, than he, if he had the power, would be justified in silencing mankind".

More recently, the author of *1984*, George Orwell argues 'If liberty means anything at all it means the right to tell people what they do not want to hear". The price of freedom is eternal vigilance.

Unlike totalitarian regimes including Russia, China, Iran and North Korea where free speech is denied and any who disagree face fines, violence, imprisonment and death open and free societies must embrace disagreement and debate.

Del Noce and eroticism

Spectator Flat White, 27 September 2023

Why are children and teenagers being indoctrinated with neo-Marxist inspired radical gender and sexuality theory? Why are transwomen cancelling women's rights to liberty and freedom and why are Western societies awash with graphic, dehumanising pornography 24/7?

Augusto Del Noce's chapter 'The Ascendance of Eroticism' published in *The Crisis Of Modernity* provides a detailed and persuasive account of why societies like Australia are facing an ever present threat represented by what he terms a sexual revolution.

A revolution where modesty and restraint no longer apply and where the prevailing ethos is one of sexual freedom and licentious self-expression. Much like the Greek tragedy *The Bacchae* we now live in a Dionysian world where there are no constraints as the ultimate gaol is sexual liberation.

Those old enough will remember the not so distant past when *Playboy* was sold under the counter, Michelangelo's statue of *David* was covered with a fig leaf and the play *Hair* achieved notoriety for daring to involve naked actors.

We now live in a time when the internet provides an incessant stream of every conceivable sexual act, sexting is common among school children, marriage no longer is defined as involving a man and a woman and where the Nike slogan 'if it feels good, just do it' reigns supreme.

Del Noce begins by detailing the impact of Wilhelm Reich's book *The Sexual Revolution* published in 1936. Reich, a Marxist associated with the Frankfurt School, argues capitalist society imposes control by denying one's sexual freedom.

While classical Marxism focuses on the modes and means of production and freeing the workers from economic exploitation Reich argues the oppressed will only be free when sexual liberation and self-autonomy are achieved.

Del Noce argues Reich "replaced the categories of bourgeoise and proletariat with those of advocates of repressive morality". Capitalist society imposes sexual anxiety and guilt and the way to freedom is to overthrow what is seen as a puritanical, life-denying ideology.

Given its belief gender and sexuality are God given and biologically determined and marriage is a sacrament involving a life-long union for the purpose of procreation, it's understandable why Reich denounces the Church as an instrument of the authoritarian state.

In addition to Reich, Del Noce argues the emergence of surrealism after the second world war also explains the dramatic shift in sexual mores and practices. Del Noce quotes one of the advocates of surrealism André Breton as arguing the sexual revolution will replace:

> *...the abominable notion of Christian sin, of original fall, of redeeming love, to replace them without hesitation with the idea of a divine union of man and woman... Morality based on the exaltation of pleasure.*

Del Noce suggests the heady counter-cultural days of the late 60s and early 70s epitomised by the emergence of the hippy movement, Woodstock, the revolt against established authority and the arrival of the birth control pill also explain why society has become libertine in nature.

Add the emergence of the gay right's movement, second wave feminism involving Betty Friedman and Germaine Greer and John Money's transgender research at John Hopkins University and it's understandable why society has undergone such a seismic shift in sexual morality.

While there are other reasons explaining the West's sexual revolution, including technological and medical innovations, Del Noce emphasises cultural-Marxism represented by the Frankfurt School and Wilhelm Reich's *Sexual Revolution.*

A striking example proving this thesis is the Safe Schools gender fluidity program widely circulated to Australian schools over the last 20 years. One of its co-designers, Roz Ward, argues the program is "about supporting gender and sexual diversity, not about stopping bullying".

Ward goes on to say, "Marxism offers both the hope and the strategy needed to create a world where human sexuality, gender and how we relate to our bodies can blossom in extraordinary, new and amazing ways that we can only try to imagine today".

Such is the pervasive influence of radical gender and sexuality theory the *Welcome to Sex* guide directed at "teens of all genders" includes topics like anal and oral sex, fingering, sexting, scissoring and details about sexual and gender fluidity.

Primary and secondary students are told sexuality and gender are social constructs and not biologically determined, that they have the power to self-identify as non-binary and that Australian society is heteronormative, homophobic and transphobic.

Such is the dominance of the neo-Marxist inspired sexual revolution that in Victoria parents, priests, doctors and health workers face fines if they counsel children and teenagers against transitioning and in Tasmania it's possible to change the gender on your birth certificate.

In 'The Ascendance of Erotism', published in 1970, Del Noce argues he was now living in a time when the average man "accepts without any moral reaction displays of sexuality that a few years ago were inconceivable". If he were alive today, he would most likely be dismayed and shocked.

Repressive tolerance: Enforcing mind control and group think

"But if thought corrupts language, language can also corrupt thought."
   — *George Orwell*

The title of this presentation draws on an essay written by the Marxist academic Herbert Marcuse in which he argues such is the oppressive and exploitive nature of Western, capitalist societies cultural-left activists have the right to employ any and all means, no matter how unacceptable, to overthrow the status quo and radically change society. Tolerance is re-defined as intolerance with Marcuse arguing "The conclusion reached is that the realisation of the objective of tolerance would call for intolerance toward prevailing policies, attitudes and opinions and the extension of tolerance towards policies, attitudes and opinions which are outlawed or suppressed". While Marcuse's essay was published in 1965, the underlying rationale and philosophy can be traced to the *Manifesto of the Communist Party* published in 1848 and written by Karl Marx and Frederick Engels.

The *Manifesto* provides a revolutionary critique of advanced, industrial Western societies and what Marx and Engels describe as "modern bourgeois society". The fathers of communism write "The history of all hitherto existing society is the history of class struggles" and "modern bourgeois society has not done away with class antagonisms. It has but established new classes, new conditions of oppression, new forms of struggle in place of the old ones".

Since the time the *Manifesto* was published the left's attack on Western societies has become more strident and all encompassing. Whereas classical Marxism focuses on analysing the modes and means of production what has become known as cultural Marxism centres on a far wider analysis of society's social, political and cultural institutions and way of life. Michael Gove argues Marxism was reconceptualised as "primarily a cultural rather than an economic movement". Gove writes "In place of anger at traditional capitalism, scorn was directed at the reigning values of the West".

The Marxist academic Louis Althusser's concept of the ideological state apparatus illustrates one of the defining features of cultural Marxism. Althusser argues capitalist society maintains dominance by ensuring institutions including schools, universities, the church, family and political, legal and cultural systems enforce the ruling ideology by conditioning citizens to accept as beneficial what is exploitive. As such, if the revolution is to be successful activists have to infiltrate and take the long march through the institutions.

The critique developed by Marx and Engels still dominates much of the cultural-left's analysis of Western, capitalist societies like Australia. Critics champion revolutionary change on the basis society is riven with inequality and oppression where the wealthy and privileged dominate and exploit the less advantaged and the dispossessed. Recent campaigns by LGBTIQ+ activists to re-define marriage and sexuality and the Black Lives Matter's argument society is awash with structural racism and white supremacism can be traced to the *Manifesto*.

The way what Sydney's Archbishop Fisher describes as absolutist secularism strives to banish Christianity from the public square and deny religious freedom of conscience and freedom of speech is also motivated by Marxism. The Italian Marxist Antonio Gramsci describes "socialism as the religion destined to kill Christianity".

As a result, in addition to Western societies being condemned for being classist society is attacked for being sexist, racist, heteronormative, homophobic and guilty of white supremacism and Eurocentrism. At the same time as condemning Western societies like Australia the cultural-left portrays itself as a beacon of equality, freedom and liberty. Only the left is committed to ending intolerance and discrimination and able to build a worldly utopia where all are guaranteed freedom.

History proves otherwise. Since Russia's communist revolution in 1917 Marxism under its various guises has led to oppression, violence and the starvation, torture and death of countless millions. Best illustrated by Big Brother and The Party in George Orwell's dystopian novel *1984* Marxism also stifles freedom of conscience and freedom of speech by enforcing mind control and group think. Whether rewriting history, controlling language, enforcing what Orwell describes as doublethink or denying and punishing disagreement and debate, the cultural-left is unforgiving and doctrinaire.

Such is the potency and prevalence of cultural Marxism, and its most recent iterations political correctness and cancel culture, barely a week goes by without yet another example of an idea, a book, a television show, a movie or an organisation or person being cancelled. Australian examples include the cartoonist Bill Leak for daring to reveal the dysfunctional nature of many indigenous remote communities and Archbishop Porteous, Israel Folau and Margaret Court for espousing a Christian view of marriage and sexuality. Australia's Barry Humphries has also suffered as a result of arguing against transgenderism based on the belief sexuality is biologically determined.

Significant, such is the pervasive and doctrinaire nature of political correctness and cancel culture, even those characterised as left-of-centre are under attack. The American non-gendered, radical feminist Camille Paglia writes "We are now plunged once again into an ethical chaos where intolerance masquerades as tolerance and where individual liberty is crushed by the tyranny of the group". A second example involves Bari Weiss, a journalist considered progressive and working at the New York Times, who felt pressured to resign because of the accusation she was guilty of what she describes as Wrongthink.

Additional evidence of the reaction against the inflexible nature of cultural-left censorship is the open letter signed by 150 authors, writers and public figures published in *Harper's Magazine*. After warning of the dangers of right-wing ideological conformity illustrated by Donald Trump's election as President the letter states

"But resistance must not be allowed to harden into its own brand of dogma or coercion – which right-wing demagogues are already exploiting. The democratic inclusion we want can be achieved only if we speak out against the intolerant climate that has set in on all sides".

While cancel-culture is relatively recent, the origins of the left's intolerance, especially targeting Christianity, can be traced to Lenin's argument any action, no matter how reprehensible, is justified if it furthers the revolutionary cause. When warning about the dangerous and destructive nature of Marxism the Italian philosopher and cultural critic, Augusto Del Noce, refers to Lenin's statement "Morality is whatever brings about the success of the proletarian revolution".

Such is the unethical and amoral nature of Marxism Del Noce concludes "every kind of violence, every ruse, every illegal action, every dissimulation, and every deception is licit if they are deemed to be necessary to reach the goal".

History proves how evil and destructive Marxism has been since the time of the Russian revolution. Untold millions have been imprisoned, tortured, starved and killed by Stalin, Mao and as a result of Pol Pot's return to Year Zero. Such extreme examples are in addition to Marxist inspired strategies like re-writing history, censoring debate, denying freedom of expression and enforcing language control and group think.

The tile of this Colloquium is 'Freedom of Speech and Religion – The Essence of Western Civilisation' and an essay titled 'Repressive Tolerance' by Herbert Marcuse provides the most explicit account of why Marxism and its recent off shoot cancel-culture represent an existential threat to freedom of conscience and freedom of expression. During the 1920s a number of Marxist academics established the Frankfurt School in Germany dedicated to championing cultural-Marxism as a way to infiltrate and take control of the West's cultural and social institutions. Along with many other academics involved, including Theodore Adorno and Wilhelm Reich, Marcuse argues Western, capitalist societies are corrupt and guilty of oppressing the marginalised and disadvantaged. In particular, Marcuse argues the existence of tolerance in Western societies "strengthens the tyranny of the majority".

As a result, Marcuse argues "what is proclaimed and practiced as tolerance today, is in many of its most effective manifestations serving the cause of oppression". As noted by Jennifer Oriel in her chapter in *Cancel Culture and the Left's Long March*:

> *Marcuse argued for a new form of inequality won by censoring dissent. He wrote a "subversive majority" could be established by "undemocratic means" including "the withdrawal of toleration of speech and assembly" from groups that dissented from left-wing politics. He proposed "rigid restrictions on … educational institutions" and "intolerance toward scientific research" that did not support his proposed revolutionary aims.*

During the late 1960s and early 1970s Western nations experienced a cultural revolution exemplified by rise of the youth counter-culture movement, Vietnam moratoriums, the birth control pill, sexual liberation and the emergence of a rainbow alliance of radical philosophies and theories. Such theories, including postmodernism, deconstructionism and post-colonial, gender and sexuality theories, represent a strident and pervasive attack on Western civilisation and societies like Australia.

While often in disagreement what all hold in common is the belief rationality and reason no longer apply as such concepts are Eurocentric, binary and instrumental in oppressing the 'other'. In the same way tolerance is condemned as part of the state's ideological apparatus employed to reinforce power and privilege; civility and objectivity are also criticised as reinforcing inequality and injustice. As a result, free and open discussion and debate are replaced by language control and group think. Much like Orwell's dystopian novel *1984*, where Big Brother and the Party rule, any who question or challenge the prevailing orthodoxy are silenced. Critical reasoning, once taught in schools as clear thinking, is replaced by emotion, hyperbole and ad hominem attacks and freedom of conscience and freedom of expression cancelled. As argued Christopher Lasch:

> *Once knowledge is equated with ideology, it is no longer necessary to argue with opponents on intellectual grounds or to enter into their point of view. It is enough to dismiss them as Eurocentric, racist, sexist, homophobic – in other words, as politically suspect.*

As damaging is the reality, once rationality and reason no longer apply and freedom of expression denied, the only alternatives are epistemological suicide or violence. Evidence such is the case includes the increasing prevalence of what Orwell calls Doublethink – described as accepting two ideas at once without realising they are contradictory. Such is the power of indoctrination and mind control in the world of *1984* citizens accept without question "war is peace, freedom is slavery and ignorance is strength".

Marcuse's argument equating tolerance with intolerance is yet another example of doublethink as is the argument the best way to promote liberty and freedom is to cancel any who think differently and who fail to conform. If it's impossible to settle arguments and disagreements rationally and by being objective and impartial it's also true violence is often the alternative. As argued by Mao "political power grows out of the barrel of a gun".

There's no doubt cancel culture is increasingly prevalent but, at the same time, there is evidence more and more people and various organisations are reasserting the primacy of rational argument and debate based on reason, logic and civility. In Australia, the Sydney based Campion College and the Ramsay Centre for Western Civilisation are committed to education being impartial and objective and teaching students the value of critical thinking and reasoned dialogue and debate. In America there are numerous liberal/arts colleges dedicated to the same objective and bodies like the Heterodox Academy and the National Association of Scholars are also beacons of common sense. In England, academics including Frank Furedi,

Douglas Murray and the late Roger Scruton have entered the public square in their campaign to warn about the dangers of doctrinaire group think and the failure to tolerate dissenting opinions.

Given the often extreme and unforgiving nature of cancel-culture it is also true more and more citizens are becoming aware of the dangers of Woke ideology. A 2019 national survey organised by the ABC found 68% of those who responded felt political correctness had gone too far. Such is the influence of cancel-culture a third survey titled 'Measuring Social Inclusion' found 3 in 5 respondents believe white Australians are victims of discrimination to some extent. In 2022 a survey managed by Mark McCrindle found one-in-four Australians are afraid to freely express themselves in relation to controversial issues including abortion, religion and the environment.

The above essay is based on a presentation given at Hobart's The Christopher Dawson Centre's Colloquium 16 July 2022 and published in Reclaiming Freedom Modern Threats to Speech & Religion. Edited by David Daintree.

Time for conservatives to call out cancel culture

Daily Telegraph, 11 July 2023

The recent survey carried out by academics at the Western Sydney University showing students found the ANZAC story irrelevant and of little interest should not surprise. An earlier survey by the Institute of Public Affairs, where 40 % of young people said they would not defend Australia if attacked, also shows schools no longer teach national pride.

Those old enough will remember the time when government schools had a picture of the Queen in the office foyer outside the principal's office and Monday morning assembly began with taking the oath of allegiance, "I love God and my country, I will honour the flag, I will serve the Queen and cheerfully obey my parents, teachers and the law."

Fast forward to more recent times and it's obvious how much has changed in terms of what is happening, or not happening, in schools. Flag raising ceremonies are passé and 'Welcome to Country' has replaced the 'Oath of Allegiance'.

The Australian national curriculum has long since jettisoned a balanced and impartial approach to history and civics and citizenship. The history curriculum embraces what Geoffrey Blainey describes as a black armband view where the arrival of the First Fleet is described as an invasion leading to genocide.

Ignored is the *King James Bible* and Blackstone's *Commentaries on the Laws of England* that arrived with Captain Phillip and that underpin the freedoms and liberties we take for granted.

The way civics and citizenship is treated in the national curriculum also highlights how successful the cultural-left has been in its long march through the institutions. An early draft of the civics curriculum tells students "Citizenship means different things to people at different times and depending on personal perspectives, their social situation and where they live".

The national curriculum, instead of acknowledging the nation's British, Irish and Scottish heritage, describes Australia as a "secular democracy and pluralist, multi-faith society (that) draws upon diverse cultural origins". Cultural relativism prevails instead of nation building and promoting social cohesion and stability.

The national curriculum undermines pride in what it means to be Australian. While the most recent iteration of the curriculum mentions *Magna Carta,* the Westminster form of government, common law and the fact we have a constitutional monarchy – all the above can be ignored by teachers in schools as none of it is compulsory.

That schools will continue to teach a black armband view of history and the nation's political and legal systems is assured given the cultural-left dominates tertiary education – including teacher training.

Given the impact of the Black Lives Matter movement and post-colonial theory trainee teachers are taught Western societies like Australia are structurally racist, Eurocentric and riven with white supremacism.

The origins of Woke ideology and cancel-culture can be traced back to the establishment the Frankfurt School in Germany during the 1920s. The British conservative politician Michael Gove argues this was a time when Marxist academics concluded the most effective way to overthrow capitalism was to start the culture wars.

Instead of focusing on inciting a communist revolution as occurred in Russia and China the focus became one of infiltrating and taking control of institutions including schools, universities, the church and families. The cultural revolution of the late 60s epitomised by Vietnam moratoriums and the rise of neo-Marxist critical theory have also had a profound effect on what is happening in schools and universities.

As a result of cultural-Marxism's dominance we now live in a world where identity politics prevails and disadvantaged individuals and groups are always presented as victims made powerless by an oppressive Eurocentric, capitalist system.

Rather than relying on reason and rationality arguments are subjective and based on emotion leading, in the end, to either epistemological suicide or violence. Instead of the Enlightenment's focus on sound argument generations of young people espouse the belief 'I feel, therefore I'm right'.

Free and open discussion and debate are replaced by what Camille Paglia describes as, "an ethical chaos where intolerance masquerades as tolerance and where individual liberty is crushed by the tyranny of the group".

What's to be done? Conservatives and those committed to rationality and reason must be willing to call out the true nature of cultural-left ideology and have the courage to be true to their beliefs and convictions.

Cultural warriors must also reassert the significance and importance of the Anglosphere and the debt we owe to the United Kingdom and Western civilisation more broadly that can be traced back to ancient Greece and Rome.

Conservatives must mobilise and organise like-minded individuals and associations and be active in the public space and take a medium to long term view of the struggle against nihilistic and destructive cultural-Marxist ideology.

Getting to the truth of the transgender theory debate

Catholic Weekly, 9 April 2023

The Moira Deeming affair, where a Victorian Liberal member of parliament was threatened with expulsion from the parliamentary party room, centres on defending women's rights given the impact of radical transgender theory.

While transwomen, biological men who self-identify as women, argue they should be treated the same as biological women Deeming argues the opposite. Human biology is such the overwhelming majority of babies are born either female (XX chromosomes) or male (XY chromosomes).

In the same way JK Rowling, Barry Humphries and Germaine Greer argue men will always be men and it's wrong for transwomen to use female changing rooms, showers and toilets, Deeming argues women's private spaces, especially for young girls, must be protected.

In response to speaking at a 'Let Women Speak' rally on the steps of the Victorian parliament, where a group of men gate crashed displaying the Nazi salute, the leader of the opposition John Pesutto argued Deeming must be punished for her supposedly transphobic, far-right views.

Lost in all the publicity and noise about whether Deeming should be punished or not is the wider and more significant debate surrounding the nature and impact of transgender theory and whether it undermines God's law and the binary nature of human biology.

The recently released doctrinal note 'Doctrinal Note on the Moral Limits to Technological Manipulation of the Human Body' by the America Committee of Doctrine leaves the reader in no doubt about the position Catholics should adopt.

The American Catholic Bishops, while accepting the strengths and benefits of modern technology, warn against "interventions that are injurious to the true human flourishing of the human person".

In particular, the Bishops argue "there is an order in the natural world that was designed by the Creator" and that an essential aspect of this natural order is a "body-soul unity" that should not be violated.

The Doctrinal Note argues each person is made in the likeness of God and, in response to the argument gender and sexuality are fluid and limitless social constructs, that "Being man or being women is a reality which is good and willed by God".

In opposition to the belief each person owns his or her own body and has the right to undergo any type of medical intervention or procedure the American Bishops quote Pope Pius XII's argument a patient "is not the absolute master of himself, of his body or his mind. He cannot dispose of himself just as he pleases".

The only time medical intervention should be allowed, according to the doctrinal note, is in order to "repair a defect in the body" or when "the sacrifice of a part of the body is necessary for the whole body".

According to the American bishops employing puberty blockers and life changing surgery in an attempt to change a person's biological sex is "not morally justified" as it fails to conform to the above criteria.

They argue such procedures are unacceptable as there "is no disorder in the body that needs to be addressed; the bodily organs are normal and healthy". Such unnatural procedures also "do not respect the fundamental order of the human person as an intrinsic unity of body and soul, with a body that is sexually differentiated".

Victoria's Moira Deeming and the American Catholic Bishops are not the only ones questioning the validity of transgenderism. While President Biden describes it as "close to sinful" over the last year a number of American states, in particular Florida, have legislated to restrict teaching gender ideology in schools and enforced safeguards to protect children from taking puberty blockers and undergoing surgery.

In the United Kingdom, the Tavistock gender clinic was closed after a report questioned its failure to properly warn children and teenagers about the dangers involved in gender transitioning. Some 1000 families are now suing the clinic for malpractice.

While in Australia hospitals still allow young people suffering gender dysphoria to take puberty blockers and undergo surgery in Europe a number of countries have warned against the practice. The Swedish National Board of Health and Welfare and the French National Academy of Medicine both argue medical intervention is not the solution.

Events overseas are in contrast to Victoria under Premier Dan Andrews where the government has legislated to impose fines and imprisonment on any, including parents, doctors, health workers and priests, who counsel young people about the dangers of transitioning.

Victoria is also the original home of the neo-Marxist inspired gender fluidity Safe Schools program teaching primary and secondary school students boys can be girls and girls can be boys and they have the right to self-identify anywhere on the LGBTIQA+ spectrum. Such ideology ignores human biology as well as the God given nature of human sexuality.

Culture, not science or scepticism, will fulfil us

Catholic Weekly, 26 March 2023

One of the most insidious and destructive aspects of Marxism and its recent manifestations cultural-Marxism and absolutist secularism is how the end always justifies the means and how any sense of the spiritual and the transcendent is lost.

Add the impact of what the Italian philosopher Augusto Del Noce condemns as "scientism and the technological society" and it should not surprise we now live in a soulless world ruled by what is utilitarian, pragmatic and self-seeking.

For those committed to Marxism and cultural-Marxism religion is condemned as the opium of the masses and any sense of the spiritual and mystical must be abolished if capitalism is to be overthrown and the workers' paradise achieved.

Instead of being free, workers are enslaved and as argued by *The Communist Manifesto* "they have nothing to lose but their chains". People are economic animals where their energy and resources must be directed at overthrowing capitalism and gaining material freedom and independence.

There is no after life as the only reality that exists is what is found on this earth. How people define themselves, find purpose in life and interact is determined by the struggle to gain liberation from the capitalist superstructure, what Louis Althusser calls the ideological state apparatus, that permeates society and controls their lives.

The City of Man replaces the City of God and it should not surprise, beginning with the French Revolution, one of the first actions taken by revolutionaries is to radically secularise society by banning religion, destroying churches and imprisoning and killing the clergy.

As detailed by Del Noce in 'Towards a New Totalitarianism' closely associated with the deadening influence of cultural-Marxism and absolutist secularism is scientism. The belief is science is "the only valid form of knowledge" and empiricism based on rationality and reason is the only way to find fulfillment, wisdom and truth.

While not denying the benefits of science, De Noce warns against what is described as a totalitarian conception of science. A restricted definition where "every other knowledge – metaphysical or religious – expresses only subjective reactions".

What cannot be proven empirically is condemned as superstition and witchcraft. Whether unravelling the mysteries of the universe, splitting the atom, putting a man on the moon or creating life invitro scientism assumes mankind is the master of his own fate.

The way nations responded to the Covid-19 pandemic by denying essential freedoms, forcing citizens to be vaccinated against their will, bankrupting businesses and shutting borders based on 'the science' proves how dangerous and counterproductive scientism has become.

The growing incidence across so-called civilised countries of euthanasia, abortion on demand and radical gender conversion therapy involving puberty blockers and life changing surgery also illustrates what happens when scientism takes control.

It's no accident, along with the denial of any sense of spirituality and transcendence, countries like Australia are suffering record rates of anxiety, depression and self-harm as well as an increasing incidence of substance abuse and societal breakdown.

In opposition to the prevailing nihilistic view of life the American academic George Weigel argues to be human is to thirst for a more sustaining sense of the world. Existential questions about the meaning of life, what constitutes fulfilment and how best to lead a moral and virtuous life cannot be answered by *Das Capital*, *The Communist Manifesto* or postmodernist theory.

Weigel in *The Cube and Cathedral* writes "the deepest currents of history are spiritual and cultural, rather than political and economic". Instead of economic determinism and nihilism Weigel argues history is driven by culture. More important than physical needs and desires is the search for what TS Eliot terms "The Peace which passes understanding".

Weigel describes this view of culture as entailing "what men and women honor, cherish, and worship; by what societies deem to be true, good and noble; by what expressions they give to those convictions in language, literature, and the arts; by what individuals and societies are willing to stake their lives on".

Similar to Weigel, Pope John Paul II in *Fides Et Ratio* makes the point to be human is to ask fundamental questions such as,

"Where have I come from and where am I going? Why is there evil? What is there after life?".

Whether Plato and Aristotle, Greek tragedies by Euripides or Sophocles, the sacred writings of Israel, the Veda and the Avesta, the writings of Confucius or the preachings of Tirthankara and the Buddha, the Pope also suggests this search has occurred throughout history and across various cultures.

The danger is we now live in a world lost in a sea of agnosticism, relativism and widespread scepticism. As argued by Pope John Paul II the challenge is to reaffirm "the path to true wisdom" in order for seekers to "find rest from their labours and joy for their spirit".

Young, free and stronger no more

Catholic Weekly, 8 January 2023

Something happened to us under restrictions of Covid – and it wasn't good for us at all.

One of the most unfortunate aspects of the way governments around the world responded to the Covid-19 pandemic was the way they imposed lockdowns, restricted people's movements and compromised essential liberties and freedoms.

Melbourne, for example, became one of the most locked-down cities in the world and those unfortunate Australians caught overseas were denied the right to return to their homeland. Grieving family members were stopped from seeing dying family and citizens forced to accept home detention.

At a speech delivered at Melbourne's Robert Menzies Institute the former Justice of the UK's Supreme Court, Lord Sumption, detailed how dangerous it was for governments to restrict citizens' freedoms and liberties and why countries like Australia are in danger of becoming authoritarian states.

Lord Sumption notes, compared to the time Menzies was Prime Minister, we now live in a time of the nanny state where, increasingly, citizens expect governments to do more and more instead of relying on their own resources.

As a result, Lord Sumption argues, "When we transfer responsibility for our well-being from ourselves to the state, we invite a much more authoritarian style of government". To illustrate this the ex-Justice notes the difference between responses to previous disasters like the Spanish flu and what occurred with Covid-19 over the last 3 years.

Citizens, instead of cherishing their freedom and being wary of government control and overreach, accepted what amounted to significant and far-reaching restrictions with barely a murmur of dissent. Referring to a 2021 Lowrey survey Lord Sumption writes, "84 per cent of Australians thought their governments had handled it (responses to the pandemic) very well or fairly well".

As to why Australians lost their sense of larrikinism and distrust of government and become so compliant Lord Sumption suggests two reasons: citizens now expect the state to do more and more instead of accepting individual responsibility and people have become increasingly risk-averse.

The resilience and self-reliance characteristic of the generation that experienced two world wars and the depression exist no longer. Citizens now expect the all-powerful state to provide and to protect them. Also gone is the time when people accepted sickness and death as a normal part of existence and it was foolish to expect they could live their lives free of suffering and pain.

When explaining why the overwhelming majority of citizens in the UK, Europe and Australia complied with draconian and unfair laws and restrictions Lord Sumption writes, "people who are sufficiently frightened will submit to an authoritarian regime which offers them security against some real or imagined threat".

Much like the way Big Brother in George Orwell's *1984* dominates and controls citizens by instilling visceral fear of the traitor Goldstein and the enemy states of Eurasia and Eastasia, governments portrayed Covid-19 as a deadly beast, unless controlled with drastic measures, that would indiscriminately kill hundreds of thousands.

In Victoria, such was Premier Andrews' success in instilling fear and convincing people only he, as the state's leader, could ensure their safety students missed a year of schooling, small businesses were bankrupted, police used rubber bullets and mace, parliament was shut and long-held liberties and freedoms denied.

While Australian governments' responses to the recent emergence of Covid-19 and its variants have been less draconian and offensive, what most concerns Lord Sumption is the reality once freedom is lost as a result of excessive and unwarranted government overreach it's very difficult, almost impossible, to regain.

After arguing "the use of political power as an instrument of mass coercion fuelled by public fear is corrosive" Lord Sumption writes, "governments rarely relinquish powers they have once acquired". As the saying goes, 'while power corrupts, absolute power corrupts absolutely'.

Proven by the existence of totalitarian dictatorships and oligarchies throughout history and those currently existing in China, Russia, North Korea, Iran and Venezuela it's obvious the liberty and freedom associated with Western liberal democracies like Australia cannot be taken for granted.

The compact between citizens and government is fragile, based on conventions, beliefs and laws often unwritten. Once trust and confidence are shattered Lord Sumption warns society descends into a Hobbesian world – one where compliant citizens are ruled by absolute governments and tyranny prevails.

As argued by Thomas Jefferson, one of America's founding fathers and statesman, "the price of freedom is eternal vigilance." Lord Sumption concludes his Menzies Institute lecture with a dire warning:

> *There is no inevitability about the future course of any historical trend. But the changes in our political culture seem to me to reflect a profound change in the public mood, which has been many years*

in the making and may be many years in the unmaking. We are entering a Hobbesian world, the enormity of which has not yet dawned on our people.

God reigns despite the darkness

Catholic Weekly, 18 December 2022

There's no doubt baby boomers born between 1946 and 1964 are now living in a very different world compared to what they experienced. Australian society, as with others in the West, has undergone a radical change making the past look like a distant and foreign land.

Radical gender theory is now taught in schools where children are told to ignore their God given, biological sex and they can decide where they fit on the LGBTIQ+ fluidity spectrum. A Christian school principal who argued otherwise was forced to resign and public figures defending the Bible cancelled.

Absolutist secularists argue Christian morals and beliefs must be banished from the public square and when deciding government policy and business organisations and government departments now enforce diversity guidelines calculated to deny the Bible's teachings.

Materialism is all pervasive where what is right and proper is measured by its utilitarian value and science and technology are lauded for giving mankind the ability to create a utopia on this earth.

Whereas pornography was once sold under the counter it is now awash on the internet, it's common for primary school children to be involved in sexting and *The Age* and *The Sydney Morning Herald* see nothing wrong in profiling a sex worker described as "one of Australia's most successful porn stars".

Whether neo-Marxist inspired gender theory, the ever increasing destructive nature of pornography and sexual exploitation, the widespread incidence of depression and self-harm or the denial of religious spirituality and transcendence there's no doubt we are living in dark times.

The works of the Italian philosopher and cultural critic, Augusto De Noce, while not widely known in Australia help to explain why we are living in what is described as a post-Christian age.

In his essay 'The Shadow of Tomorrow', published in *The Crisis Of Modernity*, De Noce argues the old forms of totalitarianism and oppression represented by communism and fascism have been superseded by what he describes as "a new, more dangerous, and more radical form of totalitarianism".

According to Del Noce, Western societies like Australia are experiencing a form of totalitarianism made up of "scientism, eroticism, and secularization" that "absolutely denies traditional morality and religion without sublimating any aspect".

While not denying the beneficial nature of science Del Noce criticises what he describes as "scientific dogmatism", a form of science that sees itself as preeminent over all other forms of knowledge and that denies the existence of anything not able to be analysed, measured and verified.

In addition to denying the significance of a spiritual view of life represented by Christianity, Del Noce argues scientism promotes a technological view of society, one that imposes a pragmatic, utilitarian view of the world and favouring the centralisation of power instead of empowering family and local community.

How governments acted in response to the Covid-19 virus proves how politicians and health bureaucrats have succumbed to scientism and a technocratic view of the world devoid of compassion and sympathy.

Government panic and overreach leading to mandatory injections, lockdowns, curfews, border closures plus closing places of worship and denying inherent liberties and freedoms were all justified by referring to the 'science'.

Illustrated by Wilhelm Reich's book *The Sexual Revolution* and the sexual freedom epitomised by the late 1960s cultural revolution, including the birth control pill and the slogan 'make love not war', Del Noce argues Western societies have undergone a revolutionary change.

A situation where "the idea of indissoluble monogamous marriage and other ideas related to it (modesty, purity, continence)" have been negated and where "It does not make sense to speak of sexual perversions; on the contrary homosexual expressions, either masculine or feminine, should be regarded as the purest form of love".

Pictures of the commonwealth members of parliament and visitors in the public gallery celebrating ecstatically after the same-sex marriage legislation was passed and the continued attacks on the nuclear family prove how prescient Del Noce was.

Illustrated by events in Victoria, where Andrew Thorburn was forced to resign as head of the Essendon football club, the anti-abortion MP Bernie Finn was expelled from the Liberal Party and a candidate for the recent election condemned for attending a Christian church, absolutist secularism is rampant.

With Christmas approaching many primary schools reject nativity scenes and Christmas carols celebrating the birth of baby Jesus and suburban streets and shop fronts are now emblazoned with decorations and images of Father Christmas and reindeers instead of the nativity scene.

There's no doubt these are dark times, but not all is lost. The birth of Jesus, his teachings and his crucifixion and ascent to heaven tell us we are not forsaken and in God's grace there is eternal peace and salvation. A Christmas message that should never be ignored or forgotten.

Oppression of our own big brother

Herald Sun, 4 November 2022

A report investigating how governments responded to the Covid-19 pandemic criticises mismanagement and over-reach.

Even more frightening and unsettling is the way Premier Daniel Andrews, with the help of health experts and the media, trashed essential liberties and freedoms while ensuring citizens remained malleable and compliant.

Even though Victoria is a Western liberal democracy where citizens' rights are protected, in response to the pandemic Andrews enacted legislation, passed laws and employed state sanctioned intimidation and violence with minimal disagreement or resistance.

Citizens have been forced to vaccinate against their will or lose their jobs and the government imposed inflexible and unnecessary lockdowns, denied free speech and freedom of assembly and threatened people with imprisonment for sitting in an empty park or walking on an isolated beach.

As a result of border closures Victorian citizens were denied the right to return home and grieving families stopped from visiting terminally ill loved ones. In scenes usually associated with third world dictatorships peaceful demonstrators have been fired upon with rubber bullets and covered with capsicum spray.

One of the techniques employed by totalitarian regimes to enforce and maintain power and ensure citizens are compliant is to employ what the Belgium psychologist Mattias Desmet describes as mass formation psychosis.

In his book *The Psychology of Totalitarianism* Desmet describes mass formation as "a kind of group hypnosis that destroys individuals' ethical self-awareness and robs them of their ability to think critically".

To ensure compliance people must be presented with an existential threat so demonised and feared the only remedy is to accept extreme measures no matter how unacceptable or unsettling.

People are conditioned to give up once accepted freedoms and liberties for the greater good and such is the overwhelming climate of fear any who question or fail to comply are beyond the pale and must be punished.

Extreme government actions are always justified for being in the people's best interests and politicians present themselves as caring and concerned guardians of public safety and order.

Desmet argues, in response to Covid-19, the way governments around the world instilled fear and anxiety to justify lockdowns and imposed draconian laws and regulations illustrates mass formation psychosis in action.

Victoria under the reign of Andrews provides an exemplary case study. Much like the 2 minute hate sessions detailed in 1984, where Goldstein is the enemy feared by all and only Big Brother can ensure safety, Andrews painted Covid-19 as an imminent and deadly threat only he could address.

The pandemic was described as an insidious, unforgiving beast having the potential to infect and kill thousands within days unless dramatic action was taken including declaring on-going states of emergency, closing parliament and enforcing a ring of steel around Melbourne.

Andrews, much like Uncle Jo Stalin and the Great Helmsman Mao Zedong, in his carefully managed and controlled media events, presented a caring and concerned figure only interested in protecting the people and ensuring their health and wellbeing.

Questions regarding the 800 deaths in aged care homes, the fact the virus escaped from quarantined hotels or small businesses being bankrupted by his actions were dismissed as insensitive and thoughtless given the Premier's only concern was to ensure public safety.

Although Andrews acts unilaterally and controls all the levers of power when inquiries pointed to mismanagement and policy failure his response was to argue he was not responsible, and his only concern was to save Victoria from the terrifying disease.

As noted by Mattias Desmet, one of the most disturbing aspects of mass hysteria is the way reason and common sense give way to thoughtless emotion and irrational group-think. Victoria, once again, provides a unique example.

At the height of the pandemic's fear campaign Victorians were told by Andrews 'staying apart, keeps us together'. Much like Big Brother's 'war is peace, freedom is slavery and ignorance is strength' the slogan involves accepting two incompatible ideas even though they contradict one another.

While there was no chance of being infected, such was the all-consuming climate of fear people wore masks when driving alone and when walking empty streets.

The pervasive influence of government propaganda and the threat of intimidation and violence led to Victorians, with a few brave exceptions, much like the citizens of Big Brother's Oceania willingly giving up their long held and cherished freedoms.

The expression 'the price of liberty is eternal vigilance' illustrates democracy's fragility and how the liberties and rights so many have died to protect can easily be lost.

Proven by how Victoria so quickly descended into a totalitarian regime characterised by government manipulation, violence and overreach the battle for freedom never ends.

Dissident plumbed the future

Catholic Weekly, 4 September 2022

As noted by Cardinal Pell in his chapter in *Christianity Matters In These Troubled Times*, Aleksandr Solzhenitsyn's 1983 Templeton address presents a prescient and convincing insight into what happens when Western societies and individuals turn their back on God and embrace what he terms "Militant atheism".

When explaining the horrors, brutality and unspeakable barbarism of the two world wars and the evil nature of fascism and communism Solzhenitsyn argues the reason is "Men have forgotten God".

The author of *The Gulag Archipelago* writes, "The failings of the human consciousness, deprived of its divine dimension, have been a determining factor in all the major crimes of this century".

Solzhenitsyn, in particular, denounces communism when he argues, "the world had never before known as godlessness as organized, militarized, and tenaciously malevolent as that practiced by Marxism" where "hatred of God is the principal driving force".

In relation to the evil nature of communism the Italian philosopher Augusto Del Noce in *The Crisis Of Modernity* makes a similar point when detailing the way communism seeks to destroy Christianity and replace it with a strident and doctrinaire form of radical secularism.

A situation where, "Marx wants to achieve the complete rejection of any dependence of man on God, and so, in the first place of dependence of God the creator". De Noce also notes, under communism, "there are no moral limitations to revolutionary action" as "politics absorbs morality within itself".

Such is the denial of God's presence and the prevalence of evil Solzhenitsyn concludes, "The entire 20th century is being sucked into the vortex of atheism and self-destruction" and "the West is ineluctably slipping toward the abyss".

While communism, proven by the millions starved, tortured and killed, is often cited as the chief threat to Christianity, Solzhenitsyn also argues, "The gradual sapping of strength from within is a threat to faith that is perhaps even more dangerous than any attempt to assault religion violently from without".

Although spoken 39 years ago it's evident Solzhenitsyn's critique is even more relevant now than when it was first presented. Communist Russia has embarked on an illegal, brutal and devasting attack on the Ukraine and China's Xi Jinping's global campaign to achieve communist hegemony threatens global security and peace.

In Russia and China, as well as other totalitarian regimes including Afghanistan, North Korea, China and Iran, Christians are denied the ability to enact their faith with thousands imprisoned or killed, churches destroyed and priests and nuns threatened and denied the ability to care for their flock.

As argued by Wanda Skowronska, one of the other authors contributing to *Christianity Matters*, "Christians are the most widely targeted religious communities in the world" suffering ever increasing rates of "internal dislocation, exodus and martyrdom".

As well as warning about the external threat represented by godless communism, Solzhenitsyn is also correct when suggesting Western societies like Australia are threatened and undermined by enemies within.

Such is the dominance of what Solzhenitsyn describes as militant atheism (inspired by Marxist ideology) we now live in a society where morality is defined by what is practical and utilitarian and the highest good is self-satisfaction and unrestricted personal freedom.

Whether the absence of any sense of the spiritual and transcendent, the overriding emphasis on materialism and the endless pursuit of happiness and immediate gratification, Christianity is no longer viewed as significant, beneficial or essential.

As a result, we now have state sanctioned killing of the old and infirm, abortions being commonplace and used as a form of birth control and the state legislating to deny religious freedom.

In Victoria the government led by the socialist-left's Daniel Andrews bans parents, priests and counsellors from cautioning teenagers and children about trying to change their sexuality. Across Australia, governments plan to abolish the right religious bodies and organisations have to decide who they employ and, with schools, who they enrol.

It should not surprise according to the 2021 national census mental health is number one on the list of most reported health conditions. Given the high rates of alcohol and drug abuse and self-harm, especially among the young, it's obvious society lacks the resilience, confidence and succour provided by God's eternal love and grace.

While Solzhenitsyn paints a dismal picture of the West he also acknowledges Christianity's ability to endure privation and hardship when he writes "But, as is always the case in times of persecution and suffering, the awareness of God in my country has attained great acuteness and profundity".

The thirst for spiritual comfort, the need to address existential questions about the meaning of life, what happens after death and how best to serve and comfort one another and to do what is good and right is never lost.

Kooyong and Wentworth: the nowhere lands

Spectator Flat White, 22 May 2022

There's no doubt Prime Minister Scott Morrison's perceived arrogance, the small target strategy employed by the ALP, and the success of the Teal faux-independents in convincing voters the world was facing an environmental apocalypse unless Australia adopted Net Zero by 2030 helps explain why Anthony Albanese is the nation's next Prime Minister.

Equally as important – especially when understanding why the Teals were successful in winning blue ribbon Liberal seats while many outer urban, regional, and country electorates stayed conservative – is Australian society is now divided between what the British author David Goodhart describes as the Somewheres and Anywheres.

According to Goodhart those in the UK who voted to leave Europe are Somewheres, that is, voters living primarily in working-class urban and regional communities who identify with family, their local community and a strong sense of British identity and values.

Anywheres, on the other hand, are affluent, well-educated city dwellers with a cosmopolitan and global outlook. Such voters shun conservatism and see any who disagree as parochial, xenophobic, and backward-looking.

The division between Somewheres and Anywheres explains why Kooyong, once held by Sir Robert Menzies and Andrew Peacock and considered the jewel in the crown of Liberal seats, is now represented by a Teal whose campaign slogan began and ended with Climate Action.

Other once safe Liberal seats – including Melbourne's Goldstein and Higgins, plus Sydney's Wentworth and North Sydney – have also fallen to Teal candidates whose campaign strategy was to argue Australians must stop being selfish, parochial, and commit to stopping global warming.

For the Teals and their often wealthy, privileged supporters it is irrelevant Australia only emits approximately 1.3 per cent of carbon emissions globally with some scientists querying the doomsday scenario. To the Teals those who question anthropomorphic climate change are denounced as ignorant and reactionary.

Living an affluent and indulged lifestyle involving expensive designer clothes, overseas holidays, private schools, European cars, and high-end restaurants, the majority of those voting for the Teals don't have to worry about the rising cost of gas and electricity or the strain on household budgets caused by the ever-increasing cost of living. Evidenced by the election result the irony is that those in the Liberal Party who argue the way to electoral victory is to appeal to the Anywheres voters by making the party of Menzies more politically correct have been proven wrong.

Even more ironic, it's the more progressive members of the Liberal Party, like Trent Zimmerman in North Sydney, who have lost their seats. Proving the maxim, it's useless for a conservative party to try and appease the Woke by copying its cultural-left agenda.

As to why Anywheres now dominate electorates like Kooyong and Wentworth look no further than the education system. The expression politics is downstream of culture makes the point it's the broader culture influencing politics. And if politics is downstream of culture then culture is downstream of education.

It shouldn't surprise the Teals chose to focus on climate change and the environment as key election issues. Since the late 60s and early 70s the threat of a nuclear holocaust has been replaced by environmental alarmism with books like *Limits to*

Growth and *Silent Spring*. The books argue unless drastic action is taken the world is doomed and students will have no future.

Illustrated by Al Gore's *An Inconvenient Truth*, which was circulated to schools 15 years ago warning about the end of the world unless fossil fuels were banned and coal mines shut, young people have long been indoctrinated with global warming alarmism.

The national curriculum embraces sustainability and the environment as one of the three cross-curricula priorities and teacher professional bodies like the Australian Education Union endorse students wagging school and striking to stop climate change.

Add to climate alarmism is the way students are taught society is inherently sexist and most men are dangerous. It should not surprise why the Teal candidates were all women standing against men and why Scott Morrison was portrayed as a misogynist.

Schools have long since jettisoned teaching clear thinking and the importance of basing arguments on logic and sound research. Student agency now rules where emotion has replaced critical thinking and any who fail to conform to cultural-left group think are ostracised and excluded.

The challenge faced by the Liberal Party is how to respond to its defeat and how to reposition itself to ensure electoral success in three years. Proven by the election results in once safe conservative seats the answer is not to out-Woke the Woke.

Instead, the party of Menzies needs to reaffirm its core values and beliefs and adopt a policy platform based on small government, protecting families and small businesses and ensuring inherent rights like freedom of religion are guaranteed.

Wokeism: the next big religion

Spectator Flat White, 31 March 2022

One of the more intriguing aspects of neo-Marxist inspired Wokeness, notwithstanding its avowed secular nature and hostility to Christianity, is how it embraces many of the characteristics of the religion it seeks to destroy and replace.

The teenage Greta Thunberg is worshipped as a new-age messiah and it's an article of faith the world is about to end because of man-made global warming. Climate sceptics are denounced as evildoers and banished to the outer regions.

Watch the young climate change novitiates demonstrating outside the Prime Minister's Sydney residence last week and, like the puritan girls depicted in Arthur Miller's *The Crucible*, it's obvious they are consumed by a religious fervour that is overwhelming, all-consuming, and driven by hysteria.

Similar to Christianity, Woke activists also have their martyrs including George Floyd and the countless other people of colour oppressed and victimised by an inherently racist society guilty of a multitude of sins including Euro-centrism and white supremacy.

Instead of the 12 disciples and the myriad Christian saints the Church of Woke immortalises and worships revolutionary figures such as Che Guevara, Ho Chi Minh, Castro, Mao and before them Stalin, Lenin, Marx and Engels.

Like Christianity, which incorporates various denominations and faiths, Woke religion also includes numerous beliefs and ideologies ranging from cultural Marxism to deconstructionism, postmodernism, radical feminism along with gender, queer, and post-colonial theories.

Instead of the Bible neo-Marxist cultural warriors worship *Das Kapital* as their foundation document supplemented by more recent works including Wilhelm Reich's *The Sexual Revolution*, Simone de Beauvoir's *The Second Sex*, Foucault's *The History of*

Sexuality and The Order of Things, Derrida's *Of Grammatology* and Althusser's *Ideology and Ideological State Apparatuses*.

While often in disagreement what all cultural-left ideologies hold in common is the belief utopia can be achieved on this earth and suffering and inequality erased if only doubters and sinners repent and drink the Kool-Aid.

While adopting many of the characteristics of religion it is obvious the Bible and the word of God are diametrically opposed to neo-Marxist inspired ideology. Whereas religion stresses the importance of spirituality and transcendence Wokeness is immediately practical, worldly and utilitarian.

There is no afterlife, this world is the sum total of existence and concepts like wisdom and truth, drawing on Althusser's concept of the ideological state apparatus, are simply social constructs imposed by society's elites to disguise their dominance and control.

As argued by Augusto Del Noce, whereas religion is inherently moral with clearly defined concepts of good and evil Woke ideologies, to a greater or lesser extent, are based on the belief the end will always justify the means. De Noce writes:

> *There is no separation between ends and means since these latter are organically subordinated to whatever goal has been discerned... Hence every kind of violence, every ruse, every illegal action, every dissimulation, and every deception becomes licit if they are deemed to be necessary to reach the goal.*

Violent protests, destruction of property, abusing and victimising others and breaking the law are all permissible if considered essential to furthering the cause. As argued by Herbert Marcuse in his essay 'Repressive Tolerance', such is the evil nature of Western, capitalist societies tolerance is no longer necessary or acceptable. Marcuse writes what is needed is "intolerance against movements from the Right, and toleration of movements from the Left".

Christianity, while evolving over time, is also based on the belief there is a past worthwhile acknowledging, protecting, and supporting. An essential part of any vibrant and enduring culture is the inheritance passed on from generation to generation based on the need to promote continuity as well as change.

Pol Pot's Year Zero best illustrates how many on the cultural-left are committed to either destroying or rewriting the past to suit their ends. In *1984*, Winston's job in the Ministry of Truth also demonstrates how totalitarian regimes control the present and future by manipulating past events.

Adam Zamoyski in *Holy Madness Romantics, Patriots and Revolutionaries 1776-1871*, when detailing the radical secular nature of the French Revolution and the way Christianity was destroyed, makes the point people will always search for a deeper and more lasting sense of life.

He writes, "By destroying the credibility of traditional ways of practising faith, through feasts, rituals, and displays, they created a vacuum. Man seeks ecstasy and transcendence, and if he cannot find it in church, he will look for them elsewhere".

In 1916 the Italian communist Antonio Gramsci referred to socialism as the "religion destined to kill Christianity". While characterised as a secular ideology opposed to God's word the irony, in seeking to banish religion, is that Marxism and its most recent iteration Wokeness, adopt many of the same characteristics.

Trust me, I'm a tree

The Conservative Woman, 25 June 2022

There's no denying the fact I'm a tree. For years I was a victim of gaslighting and draconian conversion therapy imposed by insensitive and brutal parents, therapists and counsellors. Luckily, I live in Danustan (previously known as Victoria) and the premier Daniel Andrews (aka Chairman Dan) legislated to make the practice illegal. May a hundred flowers blossom and a hundred schools of thought contend.

Thanks to the ground-breaking work of LGBTIQ+ activists we all know biological determinism no longer applies.

As argued by the gender fluidity Safe Schools champion Roz Ward, since the great reset and the rise of the new world order based on neo-Marxist inspired critical theory and Woke ideology everyone has the right to self-actualise and to be true to their inner self.

Ward argues "Marxism offers both the hope and the strategy needed to create a world where human sexuality, gender and how we relate to our bodies can blossom in extraordinary, new and amazing ways that we can only try to imagine today".

Redefining gender and sexuality was only the beginning of a glorious emancipatory and liberating age. An age where the binary, inflexible and oppressive identities imposed by the capitalist ideological state apparatus and its elites no longer apply.

An age where logic and reason are finally cancelled and truth and objectivity are replaced by raw emotion and the willingness to accept individuals construct their own reality and how they relate to and perceive others and the world in which they live.

We all know gender and sexuality are binary social constructs imposed by a cis-gendered, heteronormative society committed to cancelling the 'other'. Forget biology and the fact the overwhelming number of babies are born as girls (XX chromosomes) or boys (XY).

On the grounds of equity and social justice it's no longer enough to limit the endless possibilities for self-realisation to just those on the LGBTIQ+ spectrum. The freedom genderqueer people have to self-identify as either "transboi, boydyke, third gendered, bi-gendered, multi-gendered, androgyne, and gender bender" must be extended to the non-human world.

I first started to doubt my birth sex after my unreconstructed, non-gestational, non-birthing parent read me *The Faraway Tree*. Trees became magical places that opened an exciting and imaginary world far from the harsh realities of the Eurocentric, transphobic and oppressive society to which I was assigned at birth.

The Australian children's book *Snugglepot and Cuddlepie* (since cancelled because of the unfair demonisation of the Banksia Men) also fed what became an insatiable thirst to be true to what I was destined to be.

After reading *The Lord of the Rings* trilogy and seeing the power, resilience and wisdom displayed by the Ents I realised I wanted to be exactly like them. In the battle against evil the Ents played a decisive role and I finally understood if I was to be true to myself, I had to accept the inevitable.

The benefits of being a tree are many. We all know humans are destroying the planet and in the People's Republic of Danustan trees are protected and much loved. Logging and allowing bushwalkers and off-road SUVs have long since been banned.

Destructive, exploitive practices like searching for gas and maintaining power stations fuelled by coal have also been banned and the state offers generous subsidies to turn the countryside into a green oasis where trees are deified as part of the Gaia. I will never be alone!

Having so many trees is also a plus for all those furries wanting a safe space free from the anxiety and distress caused by the uncaring, threatening speciesism so prevalent in society riven with structural injustice and discrimination.

Being out and proud as a tree is no longer cause for self-doubt and uncertainty. We now live in a society where human biology has been cancelled. Boys can be girls and girls can be boys (or any other category on the LGBTIQ+ spectrum).

It's accepted individuals have the right to identify "as being male, female, something other or in between" and, as a result, they can be either "lesbian, gay, bisexual, queer, straight or something else" including a "Transwomen, Transman, Transguy, Trannyboy, boi, Trannygirl, Trans masculine, Trans feminine, Tranz, bi-gendered, third sex, poly gendered, transbutch, transfag, trannydyke, androgyne". It's time to add self-identifying as a tree to the list!

The shame of being white

The Conservative Woman, 24 June 2021

It's no surprise Australia's 2020 Measuring Social Inclusion Survey discovered three out of five respondents believe white Australians are the victims of discrimination to some extent.

White Australians have every right to feel discriminated against. As a result of governments pushing multiculturalism, and more recently the Black Lives Matter movement and neo-Marxist inspired critical race theory, white Australians are increasingly targeted as racist and xenophobic.

Beginning when Gough Whitlam was Prime Minister (1972-75) the school curriculum has taught students Australian society is inherently racist and it is unfair to expect migrants to assimilate.

As a result, while the overwhelming majority of migrants celebrate our way of life, a sizeable minority live in ethnic enclaves and refuse to integrate into mainstream society. Even more dangerous is some support overseas terrorist organisations and see nothing wrong with violence.

Proven by the revised national curriculum it's also true Western civilisation is either ignored or seen as oppressive. While all students are made to study Aboriginal and Torres Strait Islander history and culture studying ancient Egypt, Greece and Rome is optional.

Ignored is what the historian Geoffrey Blainey describes as "the mainsprings of the civilisation most Australians inherit". While there's no doubt that indigenous people suffered as a result of European settlement it's also true students are presented with what Blainey describes as a black armband view.

Students are told to analyse the "impact of invasion, colonisation and dispossession of lands by Europeans on the First Nations Peoples of Australia such as frontier warfare, genocide, removal from land, relocation to 'protectorates', reserves and missions".

The Black Lives Matter movement and critical race theory also explain why white Australians are becoming an endangered species. BLM activists argue Western societies like Australia are characterised by structural racism and white supremacism.

As a result, over 150 academics at Sydney University refused funding to establish a centre to study Western civilisation. One Sydney University academic goes as far as arguing subjects like history, literature, art and music are guilty of "racism, sexism, classism, historical injustice and prejudice based on religion".

Cultural-Left activists argue, given the high incidence of indigenous deaths in custody, Australia's legal system is inherently racist. Ignored, as argued by Anthony Dillon in *Cancel Culture and the Left's Long March* is the evidence proving otherwise. Dillon refers to the publication *The Health of Australia's Prisoners: 2015* that states: "With just over one-quarter (27 per cent) of prisoners in custody being indigenous, and 17 per cent of deaths in custody being indigenous, indigenous prisoners were under-represented".

White men and boys are special targets of cancel culture activists and have every right to feel discriminated against. In addition to being lampooned as 'pale, male and stale', all men are characterised as misogynist and sexist.

Workplaces have become politically correct minefields where meritocracy has been replaced by positive discrimination and quotas for women and the merest suggestion of what is deemed sexist behaviour leads to dire consequences.

Whenever the evil and heinous crime of rape occurs, all men are portrayed as complicit. School programmes like Safe Schools and Respectful Relationships teach primary and secondary students there is nothing beneficial about being masculine. One school has even asked boys to stand at assembly and apologise for being male.

Such are the concerns about discrimination a group of mothers have started a Mothers of Sons website https://www.mothersofsons.info/ detailing examples of how boys are being humiliated and made to feel guilty.

Prejudice and unfair discrimination are totally unacceptable. The danger, though, in these politically correct times is not all are treated fairly and equally. In the case of white Australians, the campaign for tolerance has led to intolerance.

Fundamental flaws in gender theory

The Conservative Woman, 16 April 2021

The Australian Broadcasting Corporation (ABC) is the antipodean equivalent of the BBC, and recently on its prime current affairs show Q&A one of the Scott Morrison government's high-profile politicians, Trent Zimmerman, sounded more like a cultural-left radical than a Liberal Party politician committed to a conservative agenda.

When discussing gender and religion Zimmerman argues, "Any person should be able to decide what future they want for their own life and what they do with their body is part of that". This was in response to Martyn Iles from the Australian Christian Lobby who defended rugby star Israel Folau's condemnation of homosexuality as a sin.

According to Zimmerman every individual has the right to decide whether he or she is male, female or lesbian, gay, bisexual, transgender, etc, regardless of what medical science tells us or a person's obligations and responsibilities to others and society in general.

Zimmerman, thus, unwittingly reveals a fundamental weakness in neo-Marxist-inspired gender theory. Denying one's God-given sex by arguing gender is a social construct is a relatively recent phenomenon. The origins of radical gender theory arguing boys can be girls and girls can be boys, despite the fact that human biology proves otherwise, can be traced to Germany's Frankfurt School established in the early 1920s.

The Marxist academics associated with the Frankfurt School argued the most effective way to overthrow capitalism was to engage in the culture wars. One of these academics was Wilhelm Reich whose seminal book *The Sexual Revolution* heralded a revolutionary critique of traditional sexuality and institutions such as marriage.

During the counter-cultural revolution of the 60s and early 70s Reich's book was rediscovered and what become known as the LGBTIQ+ movement emerged as a significant global force, especially in Western societies such as Australia. At the same time the word gender was redefined from being a grammatical expression to one suggesting sexuality was fluid, dynamic and limitless.

Primarily responsible was the researcher John Monday from Johns Hopkins University in Baltimore who introduced the description gender on the basis sexuality was a social construct imposed by a straight, heteronormative society.

Ignored is the biological reality that approximately 99 per cent of babies are born as boys or girls. Not surprisingly, this explains why surveys show approximately 98 per cent of adults identify as women or men. As argued by the American College of Pediatricians, "human sexuality is an objective biological trait" and "human sexuality is binary by design with the obvious purpose being the reproduction and flourishing of our species".

It's important to note opposition to transgenderism crosses ideological boundaries. While criticism is normally associated with Christian conservatives such as Martyn Iles, the American radical feminist Camille Paglia and Australia's Germaine Greer and Barry Humphries are also very critical. Paglia argues the "DNA of every cell of the human body is inflexibly coded as male or female from birth to death".

Zimmerman's argument individuals must have the right to control their own bodies regardless of biology is also flawed as it embodies a philosophy, in the words of Pope Francis, that is "based almost exclusively on the autonomy of the individual will".

Pope Benedict also opposes gender theory when arguing denying one's birth sex destroys "the very essence of the human creature through manipulating their God-given gender to suit their sexual choices". Benedict argues, "When the freedom to be creative becomes the freedom to create oneself, then necessarily, the Maker himself is denied and ultimately man too is stripped of his dignity as a creature of God".

In the context of the New South Wales government's inquiry into the Education Legislation Amendment (Parental Rights) Bill 2020, that seeks to stop schools and teachers indoctrinating students with neo-Marxist gender theory, it is also vital to understand children and teenagers should not be granted the autonomy to decide for themselves what gender they prefer.

Parents are the primary educators and moral guardians of their children responsible for ensuring their children do not come to harm by making decisions many will inevitably regret. Normalising transgenderism, for example, is dangerous to young and vulnerable students who, for whatever reason, are experiencing gender dysphoria.

Illustrated by the recent British High Court Decision to ban puberty blockers for children under 16 the reality is young adolescents are not in a position to make critically informed and rational decisions. As argued by Professor Diana Kenny in her submission to the NSW inquiry, it is wrong to "undermine parental authority in the child's eyes, setting a dangerous precedent allowing children to make decisions about their wellbeing for which they are not emotionally or cognitively ready".

The moral void at the heart of cancel culture

The Conservative Woman, February 18, 2021

For all its posturing about taking the high moral ground and ridding society of intolerance and prejudice every now and again cancel culture activists reveal their true nature. In the context of the recent Australian debate about Victoria's legislation to ban gay conversion therapy the LGBTQ+ policy analyst Daniel Comensoli does just that.

When arguing in favour of the bill, one that makes prayer illegal in the context of conversion therapy, Comensoli argues public policy should never by influenced by "moral judgement" or "discrimination".

The Shorter Oxford Dictionary defines moral as, "of or pertaining to the distinction between right and wrong, or good and evil, in relation to actions, volitions, or character; ethical". One of the defining distinctions between a civilised and uncivilised society is the former strives to be inherently moral.

If society is to protect the life and liberty of each citizen and to ensure justice and fairness for all then moral judgement is essential. The concept of natural law and the great religions of the world, including Christianity, are based on moral precepts and when asking what constitutes the good life and a just society an ethical framework is vital.

To suggest otherwise by arguing there is no place for morality is both contradictory, on what other basis can human rights be protected, and dangerous. One of the defining lessons from history is totalitarian regimes are amoral; a situation that quickly leads to inequality, violence and terror as physical force and coercion are the only alternatives.

As argued by the Italian philosopher Augusto Del Noce in *The Crisis of Modernity* revolutionary and totalitarian regimes like communism in striving to create a worldly utopia deny "the very idea of virtue in the traditional sense" committing "every violation of the moral order for the sake of (supposed) human happiness".

Whether the rise of communism in Russia and China or Pol Pot's return to Year Zero all such movements in denying the central importance of morality create a world devoid of compassion, tolerance and a commitment to individual liberty and the common good.

While not suggesting today's cultural-left activists are anywhere near as evil as Lenin, Stalin, Mao or Pol Pot cancel culture and the political correctness movement share the same antecedents and have much in common.

Central to both is the belief it is possible to create a worldly utopia where all exist in harmony and there is no injustice and inequality. Illustrated by Marx's mantra "from each according to his ability and to each according to his needs" by overthrowing capitalism the workers' paradise would arise.

Cultural-left gender theory promises the same results as argued by Roz Ward who is one of the designers of Safe Schools. Ward argues "Marxism offers both the hope and the strategy needed to create a world where human sexuality, gender and how we relate to our bodies can blossom in extraordinary, new and amazing ways that we can only try to imagine today".

Cultural-left ideologies also advocate what Karl Popper describes as historicism, defined as "the doctrine that history is controlled by specific historical or evolutionary laws whose discovery would enable us to prophesy the destiny of man". Instead of human destiny being determined by larger, uncontrollable forces what eventuates can be foreseen and controlled.

Del Noce makes the point revolutionary movements like communism are also opposed to religion, especially Christianity. As argued by Karl Marx, "religion is the opium of the masses" and one of the first steps under communist dictatorships is silencing the church and denying Christians their faith.

Again, while not as extreme, cultural-left activists are also dedicated to a world without religious faith where public policy is decided void of any religious influence. In its submission to the commonwealth's inquiry into religious freedom the Secular Party argues "religion is a private, individual matter and religion should not impact the public square".

The Australian newspaper's Peter Van Onselen argues it's wrong to treat religious faith as a positive right as Australians are "living in a secular society". Victoria's Premier Daniel Andrews when supporting his government's draconian gay conversion therapy bill also argues there is no room for religion as "Victoria is a secular state".

Explicit in such arguments is what Sydney's Archbishop Fisher describes as "absolutist secularism". An ideology that "tries to minimise the role of religion in every person's life, to exclude it altogether from the public square, and to remove religious institutions from having any influence over government, law, media, schools, universities, the arts, workplaces, social customs, civil discourse, even the civic calendar."

Australia's Woke Education System, Dumber and Dumber

Time to take action to empower schools

Daily Telegraph, 1 February 2024

With schools returning after the Christmas break it's time to consider what the next 12 months holds for education. What happens, or does not happen, in schools is crucial not only for the ability of students to lead productive, fulfilling and rewarding lives, it also determines whether we remain a stable, cohesive and relatively prosperous nation.

Proven by the way the cultural-left has captured education to indoctrinate students with neo-Marxist inspired ideology regarding climate change, gender fluidity, toxic masculinity and the evils of Western civilisation and Christianity the future is less than optimistic.

Since the cultural revolution of the late 1960s teacher unions, subject and professional bodies and teacher training academics have succeeded in turning classrooms into re-education gulags committed to enforcing Woke mind control and group think.

Distraught teenage girls cry about not having babies because the world is about to end, kindergarten toddlers are taught girls can be boys and boys can be girls as gender is a social construct, and primary school children told to beware of toxic masculinity as society is patriarchal and misogynist.

The oath of allegiance and raising the flag have been replaced by 'Welcome to Country' and reciting the Uluru Statement and, based on the belief society is multi-racial, multi-ethnic and characterised by diversity and difference, students are no longer patriotic and proud to be Australian.

With few exceptions teachers are no longer subject experts and authority figures, instead, student agency, wellness and child-centred learning prevail where teaching the basics and essential knowledge are replaced with a process, inquiry-based approach to learning.

After 12 years of primary and secondary education generations of students continue to leave school illiterate, innumerate as well as morally and spiritually impoverished and culturally illiterate. Instead of respecting authority too many students are self-centred and unable to take advice or criticism.

Teachers and schools are overwhelmed with needless bureaucratic red-tape imposed by two levels of government and bureaucrats at head office far removed from the practicalities and realities of the classroom.

Add the fact the curriculum is overcrowded and impossible to teach and the assessment and reporting system is overly cumbersome and time consuming it's no surprise so many teachers are either leaving or planning to leave the profession.

Such is the attrition rate hundreds of schools across the state will continue to face staff shortages with teachers made to teach subjects they are not trained for and schools made to employ short term casual staff – if they can be found.

The pressure placed on teachers to be social welfare workers, child psychologists and experts in cyber-bullying, sexting and dealing with students' anxiety and depression will only add to the burden already overwhelming schools.

What's to be done? Instead of yet more inquires and reviews as planned by the commonwealth minister for education Jason Clare it's time for action. For a start the commonwealth needs to give responsibility for school education back to the states and territories.

Expensive, bloated bureaucracies including the national curriculum body ACARA and AITSL responsible for detailing teacher quality plus the research organisation AERO need to be scrapped. There are already 8 state and territory bodies doing the same job.

Teacher training needs to be overhauled to ensure beginning teachers are properly trained to be subject experts and capable of enforcing a disciplined classroom where students know what constitutes acceptable behaviour and there are consequences for breaking the rules.

Much like the teachers colleges that disappeared years ago when university faculties of education were established, we need to reduce academic theory and trainee teachers, like apprentices, must spend more time in the classroom being mentored by experienced practitioners.

Parents, instead of expecting schools to do everything and teachers being at their beck and call 24/7 need to man up, take responsibility and teach their children civility, manners and that being at school is a privilege they should never take for granted.

Proven by events overseas, giving schools greater autonomy and flexibility is also a must. Like community schools that blossomed during the early 1970s schools, based on the concept of subsidiarity, need control over staffing, budgets and curriculum focus. Strengthening parental choice with education vouchers is also a winner.

Such is the disappointment with Australia's education system more and more parents and teachers are establishing their own schools. Whether Sydney's Hartford College, Brisbane's St John Henry Newman College or Melbourne's Harkaway Hills College communities are lighting small fires.

Such schools are committed to a classical, liberal education dedicated to a rigorous curriculum, teaching virtues like humility, courage and justice and ensuring classrooms are disciplined and both students and parents are committed to the school's ethos, beliefs and values.

Schools for fools: educational corruption

Daily Telegraph, 2 January 2024

Looking back over the last 12 months it's obvious schools are no longer places where students are taught in a balanced and impartial way and where teachers have a duty of care to be fair and reasonable.

Long gone are the days when teachers were the masters of their subject and saw their duty as introducing students to what Matthew Arnold describes as "the best that has been thought and said".

Instead of being taught clear thinking, where the aim is to evaluate arguments in a rational and dispassionate way, students are turned into cultural-left warriors on climate change, gender fluidity, Aboriginal history, multiculturalism and the evils of Western civilisation and Judeo-Christianity.

The national curriculum and the NSW History syllabus indoctrinate students with a black armband view of the nation's history and institutions. Instead of the arrival of the First Fleet being an incredible feat in navigation and survival students are told it led to the destruction of a pristine indigenous culture.

Ignored is the reality, as argued by David Kemp in *The Land of Dreams,* is along with the convicts, marines and Governor Phillip, was the *King James Bible* and Blackstone's *Commentaries on the Laws of England.*

Both ensured, for all its flaws and shortcomings, the convict settlement evolved into a colony based on the rule of law, the inherent rights of all citizens, parliamentary government and Christian beliefs including charity to others, doing good instead of evil and rejecting slavery.

Also ignored, proven by William Buckley's first-hand account of living with Aborigines in what is now Melbourne's Bellarine Peninsula, is before European settlement tribal warfare was common, as was cannibalism, misogyny and infanticide.

Whereas sex education once was relatively straightforward, explaining human reproduction and sexuality, in kindergartens and pre-schools children are taught gender and sexuality are fluid and dynamic social constructs.

Instead of being binary and God given students are told they have the right to decide where they fit on the LGBITQA+ spectrum and secular and faith-based schools are pressured to provide gender neutral toilets and changing rooms to accommodate trans-students.

Beginning with Al Gore's misleading and cataclysmic video *An Inconvenient Truth* and ending with the School Strike 4 Climate demonstrations, students are indoctrinated with the belief the world is about to end because of man-made climate change.

Even though Australia's contribution to global carbon emissions is just over 1 percent and countries like China and India have hundreds of coal powered stations between them students are told Australia must replace fossil fuels with costly and intermittent wind turbines and solar panels.

Indoctrinating students with the belief Australia is a multi-faith, multi-ethnic society characterised by diversity and difference further illustrates how schools have become Woke education camps.

Even though the nation's legal system, its Westminster parliamentary system, its language and much of its music, literature and art are derived from the United Kingdom, Ireland and Europe, the curriculum is based on cultural relativism where there is nothing special or unique about Western civilisation.

Whereas schools once were involved in nation building and encouraging stability and social cohesion, Australia is now fragmented and in danger of becoming what the historian Geoffrey Blainey describes as a nation of tribes.

It's not surprising so many young people are taking to the streets waving Palestinian flags, chanting 'from the river to the sea, Palestine will be free' and condemning Israel as an imperialist state illegally occupying stolen land.

Illustrated by the rise of anti-Semitism and cancel culture where intolerance masquerades as tolerance, it's clear schools fail to teach the central importance of respecting others and acknowledging all have the inherent right to liberty and freedom.

Much of the public debate over the last 12 months has centred on falling literacy and numeracy standards, teacher quality, school funding and what governments can do to raise standards and ensure a more effective education system.

Equally as vital is stopping schools from indoctrinating students with left-of-centre ideology and ensuring the curriculum presents complex and controversial issues in a balanced and objective way.

Too many students are leaving schools culturally illiterate and incapable of weighing arguments in a rational and reasoned way. The saying 'I think therefore I am' has been replaced by 'I feel, therefore I'm right'.

Instead of ideology and cant schools need to recapture the true purpose of education. An education promoting rationality and reason, that introduces students to what is best about the West's cultural heritage and that contributes to human goodness and human flourishing.

To do otherwise is to give students an impoverished and superficial education; one that denies the ability to lead a morally, spiritually and intellectually fulfilling life.

The Politics of Envy

Spectator Flat White, 20 December 2023

One of the defining moments of the 2004 federal election was Mark Latham's hit list of wealthy non-government schools and John Howard's success in describing the ALP policy as the politics of envy. Jason Clare, the Minister for Education, is making the same mistake.

In response to a recently released report titled *Improving Outcomes For All* commissioned by Clare, he argues, 'The growing gap between the rich and poor, largely as a result of segregation, based on wealth into government and non-government schools was unacceptable.'

Based on the argument that poor students are always disadvantaged, Clare also argues 'we have one of the most segregated school systems in the OECD. Not by the colour of your skin, but by the size of your parents' pay packet'.

Based on the assumption that school choice, where parents have the right to decide where their children are educated, is inequitable and unjust, Clare's report offers 10 interventions calculated to level the playing field and ensure all schools, especially non-government, embrace socio-economic diversity and difference.

Reforms include legislated quotas 'with penalties for noncompliance', stopping non-government schools from charging fees and forcing them into the state system, stopping schools from selecting students on academic ability, and offering incentives to 'quality educators' to teach in disadvantaged schools.

After admitting there is no one solution to solve the issue of segregation the report argues all schools, government and non-government, must be involved to ensure all students, regardless of postcode or wealth, 'have pathways to enrol in high-quality schooling'.

While justified in terms of equity and fairness by forcing schools to enrol students from a diverse range of home backgrounds, the report denies school choice, reduces all schools to the one level of mediocrity and state control, and stops schools charging fees and controlling who they enrol.

Since the heady days of the late 1960s, schools have been a key target in the cultural-left's long march through the institutions. Drawing on the sociology of education movement, the argument is schools are complicit in reproducing capitalist hierarchies and concepts like meritocracy are social constructs reinforcing privilege.

Drawing on cultural-Marxism, prominent academics argue schools must be captured if the socialist dream of 'from each according to his ability, to each according to his needs' is to be achieved.

Victoria's Premier, Joan Kirner, argued at a Fabian meeting, schools must be 'part of the socialist struggle for equality, participation and social change rather than in instrument of the capitalist system'.

The Australian Education Union for decades has characterised Australian society as riven with social injustice and inequality, argued Catholic and independent schools don't deserve funding, and government schools serving low socioeconomic communities must be given priority.

The flaws in Minister Clare's attack on so-called wealthy and privileged parents who choose non-government schools are manifest. International covenants and agreements endorse parental choice and argue parents must not be discriminated against because of where they enrol their children.

Given the Woke, extreme secularist nature of government schools and education departments pushing neo-Marxist inspired gender and sexuality theories, climate alarmism, critical race and postcolonial theories, plus identity politics, it is especially vital religious parents are free to choose.

Underlying the billions of dollars wasted as a result of the Gonski funding review, proven by international and NAPLAN tests results either flatlining or going backwards, is the myth a student's socioeconomic background is the key determinant explaining success or failure.

While promulgating the SES myth fits the socialist belief society is structurally classist and investing more in schools serving disadvantaged communities will remedy the problem, the reality is the opposite.

Research undertaken by one of Australia's leading education experts and psychometricians Gary Marks concludes SES accounts for 10-16 per cent when explaining outcomes. Analysis undertaken as part of the PISA test makes the same point when concluding SES contributes 15 per cent to test results.

More important factors include disciplined classrooms and setting high expectations, having a rigorous and teacher friendly curriculum, ensuring what happens in the classroom is effective and that teachers are subject experts supported by parents.

Contrary to the myth parents' wealth is the major factor, research proves student ability and motivation are also keys to educational success. Research puts the impact of genetic inheritance at between 50 to 67 per cent and explains why working-class students are not always destined to under achieving.

Attacking Catholic and independent schools also fails the financial literacy test. On average while government school students receive $20,940 in government funding the figure for students attending non-government schools is $12,442.

Parents paying non-government school fees save state, territory, and commonwealth governments billions each and every year plus their taxes also support government schools. Proven by year 12 results, it's also true non-government schools, with the exception of selective schools, consistently outperform government schools.

The Albanese government's record of electorally disastrous polices include the Indigenous Voice, rocketing energy prices caused by climate alarmism, unacceptable rates of immigration and holding small businesses to account with its union-friendly industrial relations regime. Add school choice and school funding to the list.

Education destroyed by self-serving educrats

Spectator Flat White, 8 December 2023

Such is the parlous and substandard state of Australia's education system if those in charge managed a major corporation like Qantas, Optus, or Woolworths they would either be investigated by the ACCC, be removed from the board, or have their salaries and bonuses docked.

Not so for those career educational bureaucrats, academics, subject experts, and carpetbaggers who have played a central role in the nation's dismal collapse in educational standards over the last 30 to 40 years.

Whether we look at international tests like PISA – where today's 15-year-old students are a year behind their year 2000 counterparts – university courses being dumbed down due to first year students being unable to cope, or employers complaining about illiteracy and innumeracy, Australian education is going down the gurgler.

Despite the additional billions of dollars invested as a result of the Gonski funding review, multiple national reform agreements over the last 30 years and countless government-sponsored curriculum and assessment inquiries and reviews, generations of students have been, and still are, destined to failure.

There's nothing new in the latest 2022 PISA results highlighting Australia's descent into mediocrity. In 2004 I wrote about why our schools are failing and cited evidence from tests and surveys carried out in 1975, 1995, and 1996 concluding nearly 30 per cent of primary students failed basic literacy tests.

When detailing why Australia under-performs and why standards have declined so dramatically the usual suspects include ineffective classroom practice, a superficial, substandard curriculum, lack of discipline, failure to set high expectations, and parents abrogating their responsibilities.

Rarely identified is the major systemic problem infecting Australia's education system. A problem centred on the fact those responsible over the last 30 to 40 years have failed dismally in their responsibility to provide students with a challenging, enriching, and worthwhile education.

Beginning in the early 1970s those tasked with training teachers jettisoned the more traditional approach based on teacher authority, teacher-directed lessons, rote learning and memorisation in favour of a range of progressive, new-age innovations and fads.

Open classrooms, community schools, student-centred learning, the whole word 'look and guess' approach to reading as well as diagnostic, descriptive reporting and assessment based on the belief ranking and failing students is bad for their self-esteem dominated.

Professional bodies including the Australian Council for Educational Research, the Australian Curriculum Studies Association and the Deans of Education all imbibed the educational Kool-Aid committing generations of students to failure.

The Australian Education Union, not surprising given its cultural-left leanings, argues the competitive, academic curriculum must be overthrown as it reinforces capitalist hierarchies. Ignored is forsaking meritocracy especially punishes disadvantaged but bright working class students.

In 2005 the Head of the AEU boasted such had been the success of the union's long march through the education system "the conservatives have a lot of work to do to undo the progressive curriculum".

The Australian Association for the Teaching of English is also responsible for falling standards as measured by international tests. Drawing on the neo-Marxist-inspired concept of critical literacy the AATE has long argued teachers should forsake teaching standard English and grammatically correct language in favour of empowering and liberating students by emphasising student agency and creativity.

Proven by the publication in 1998 of *Going Public: Education policy and Public Education in Australia* the Australian Curriculum Studies Association is also responsible for Australia's dumbed down, ineffective curriculum.

The book argues in favour of "social democratic values that lie at the heart of progressive aspirations about public education" and argues fears about falling standards are "alarmist and negative" spread by conservative politicians and a subservient media to undermine public education.

Against what is condemned as "reactionary policy development" ACSA calls for schools and teachers to redouble their efforts to teach an emancipatory and liberating view of education calculated to indoctrinate students with its progressive, left-of-centre ideology.

Commonwealth, state, and territory education departments and bodies like the Australian Curriculum, Assessment and Reporting Authority cannot escape blame for turning Australia's education system into an intellectual wasteland.

Multiple national education reform agreements proving ineffective and costly government and bureaucratic intervention have drowned school leaders and teachers in needless red-tape and mindless busy work contributing to burnout and high attrition rates.

Even more disturbing, based on the principle of promoting people to their least level of ability, those educrats responsible for destroying what was once a successful and rewarding education system are either promoted or recycled as members of yet another inquiry or review.

Like the old industrial relations club those responsible for Australia's educational decline are a self-serving, inward-looking coterie more concerned with power and prestige than raising educational standards.

The alternative is a market-driven system of education based on subsidiarity and parental choice represented by autonomous community schools and school vouchers.

Curriculums must ward off Woke ideology

Daily Telegraph, 24 November 2023

Proven by students wagging school to attend the School Strike 4 Climate rally and the protest organised by School Students for Palestine, it's obvious young and vulnerable students are being indoctrinated with cultural-left ideology.

Students are terrified the world is about to end due to the climate apocalypse and convinced Israel is wrong to defend itself against the barbaric and evil invasion by the Islamic terrorist group Hamas based in Gaza.

Given the way students are being weaponised as cultural-left warriors it's crucial how civics and citizenship is taught in schools is impartial and free of indoctrination and group think.

Students are the nation's future citizens and what they learn about Australia's political and legal institutions, their rights and responsibilities and the origins of freedom of speech, universal franchise, popular sovereignty, separation of powers and the rule of law is especially important.

The NSW's curriculum is currently under review and it's crucial what is taught is academically rigorous, balanced and guaranteed to ensure students leave school knowledgeable and well informed.

Those responsible for the civics and citizenship curriculum argue, "The attainment of knowledge is a key goal of education" and the new approach "outlines the essential knowledge, understanding and skills students are expected to demonstrate".

Such is not the case. Unlike the national curriculum that includes civics and citizenship as a separate subject the NSW approach integrates civics and citizenship within the Human Society and Environment K-6 syllabus, the History 7-10 curriculum and the optional Commerce subject.

As a result, students will receive a patchy and superficial knowledge of what makes Australia's political and legal institutions unique. The situation is made worse because what should be compulsory, such as ancient Greece's contribution to democracy and the evolution of the West's legal system since ancient Rome and the rise of Christian Europe, are optional.

While it's good the draft curriculum asks students to study "the role Christianity played in laying the political, social and cultural foundations of post-Roman European societies collectively known as Christendom", there's no guarantee it will be taught.

Students can leave school after studying ancient China or ancient India without any substantial knowledge or appreciation of the origins of Western, liberal democracies like Australia that are underpinned by a Westminster inspired parliamentary and legal system and Judeo-Christianity.

As argued by the Rule of Law Education Centre's submission to the draft curriculum, another problem is key concepts such as the rule of law, separation of powers and *Magna Carta* are either ignored, treated superficially or are voluntary.

While significant political philosophies including liberalism, nationalism, imperialism, democracy, socialism, communism and revolution are included in the draft the problem is teachers have only a mere 10 hours to cover all the content.

Add the fact teachers are also supposed to teach the rise of European nation states, the industrial revolution and the impact of colonisation, imperialism and patterns of global conflict 1918-1939 and its obvious the syllabus is overcrowded and impossible to teach.

While those responsible argue the NSW syllabuses cover less content than the national curriculum the opposite is the case. Teachers are still pressured to cover too much detail in too short a time.

Another criticism levelled by the Rule of Law Education Centre is the undue emphasis on Aboriginal history and culture to the exclusion of Australia's mainstream political and legal institutions and history.

While students are made to describe "Aboriginal Cultures, Knowledge and Histories for an understanding of Australia" and identify "key events in Aboriginal histories of Australia" the same cannot be said of the nation's debt to Western civilisation and its evolution as a Western, liberal democracy.

The Education Centre argues students "will have an excellent understanding of the Aboriginal history, culture and experience, and almost no understanding of basis of the Australian system of government under which they live, and how that contributes to Australia being a free, democratic and egalitarian country".

The American President Abraham Lincoln argues "the philosophy of the schoolroom in one generation will be the philosophy of the government in the next". What students learn or don't learn is a major influence on how they will act and think as citizens.

It's vital those responsible for teaching the next generation of citizens, including teachers and school leaders plus subject associations and education minsters, ensure education is free of Woke ideology.

The civics and citizenship curriculum must be academically rigorous and impartial, ensuring students leave school as critically aware, independent and rational thinkers. The draft NSW K-6 and 7-10 syllabuses fail in this regard and make students more vulnerable to cultural-left mind control and group think.

Much still to be done to sort out this mess

Daily Telegraph, 25 August 2023

Read the headlines in response to the latest National Assessment Plan Literacy and Numeracy (NAPLAN) results for years 3, 5, 7 and 9 and you would be shocked and appalled so many Australian students under-perform and are educationally at risk.

One headline reads "One third of Australian students fail to meet the new NAPLAN benchmarks", another shouts "After radical overhaul, one-third of students fail to meet NAPLAN standards" while yet another states "$662bn debacle: one in three kids fails NAPLAN literacy, numeracy".

Despite all the talk about an educational crisis there is nothing new about the latest NAPLAN results. In *Why our schools are failing* published in 2004 I wrote the 1996 national literacy test showed approximately 27% of year 3 students and 30% of year 5 primary school children were illiterate.

I also wrote, based on the results of a Longitudinal Study of Australian Youth carried out by the Australian Council for Educational Research in 1995, 30% of Australian students failed the literacy test. International tests provided further evidence Australian students underperformed compared to overseas students.

At the time I was condemned by Australia's education establishment as a Cassandra guilty of exaggerating the issue and talking up a literacy and numeracy crisis that supposedly did not exist.

In her book *The Literacy Wars* Ilana Snyder also criticised the then John Howard government and the Murdoch press for arguing Australia's education system had been dumbed down as a result of adopting new-age, progressive fads.

History tells us who was correct. Australia' school education system, despite the additional billions invested and despite a plethora of national reform agreements, teacher training and curriculum reviews plus state and territory reforms, is still mired in mediocrity and falling standards.

Over the last 20 to 30 years it's also true boys have especially suffered when it comes to reading and writing with girls consistently outperforming boys as a result of teaching methods and a curriculum calculated to discriminate in their favour.

It's not just substandard literacy and numeracy results as measured by NAPLAN and international tests including PISA and TIMSS signifying how bad the situation is. Australian classrooms are among the noisiest and most disruptive across the OECD countries.

Overworked and stressed teachers are leaving the profession in droves and teaching as a career is no longer seen as a worthy pursuit. Schools and school leaders, as a result of two levels of government enforcing a top down, bureaucratic approach, are drowning in red tape.

Add the fact too many parents fail to instil in their children respect for others, especially authority figures like teachers, and a love of learning and the need to strive to achieve and no wonder teachers are doing it hard and schools no longer perform as they should.

Too many parents, instead of talking and interacting with their children from an early age and introducing them to picture books, also make the mistake of using computer and mobile screens to entertain their children.

What's to be done? One approach, illustrated by the commonwealth minister for education Jason Clare, is to announce yet more teacher training and curriculum reviews as well as implementing a new national reform agreement.

The only problem is the very institutions and many of the so-called experts chosen by Clare are the ones responsible for the current mess. Dracula is in charge of the blood bank and as the saying goes – it's rare those responsible for a problem are the ones best able to remedy it.

It's also obvious schools, instead of having the autonomy and flexibility to best manage their own affairs, will still have to conform to educational mandates delivered on high and tied to funding.

Proven by the popularity and success of America's charter schools and England's city academies and free schools what schools need is control over who they employ, their work conditions, curriculum focus and the ability to best reflect the needs and aspirations of their communities.

Parents also need greater school choice by introducing school vouchers. Over 14 states in the USA have implemented school vouchers, including Florida, Mississippi and Milwaukie, and such has been their success, especially in disadvantaged urban areas, schools are over enrolled.

Giving parents a voucher, often equivalent to the cost of educating a student to what is defined as a reasonable standard of education, allows them to better choose a school that best suits their child as well as pressuring schools to achieve stronger outcomes.

While there is no doubt literacy and numeracy are education's building blocks, it's also vital any curriculum is content rich, academically rigorous and emotionally, morally and spiritually sustaining.

There is a right time and place for sex education

Daily Telegraph, 16 August 2023

It shouldn't surprise so many mothers campaigned against Target, Dymocks and Big W for selling the children's book *Welcome to Sex* and Big W, while still selling it online, withdrew the book from its stores.

The book, written by Dr Melissa King and Yumi Stynes and styled as a "frank, age appropriate introductory guide to sex and sexuality for teens of all genders", includes topics like anal and oral sex, fingering, sexting, scissoring and sexual and gender fluidity.

While sex education generally deals with basic facts about conception, reproduction and human sexuality what *Welcome to Sex* provides, as well as graphic images of naked men and women in various positions, is a manual about how to engage in various sexual activities.

Especially controversial is the page about sexting where children are told if they email naked images of themselves, they should cover their faces. Ignored is the cyber safety expert Susan McLean's argument texting naked images opens children to possible criminal charges.

What parents have to realise is *Welcome to Sex* is not the only book guilty of sexualising children and teenagers. Even more extreme is *Let's Talk About It* by Erika Moen and Matthew Nolan. Described as a "graphic novel about sex, sexuality, gender and many other topics for teens" topics include gender, sexuality, masturbation plus kinks, fantasies and porn. The section on masturbation is especially graphic with boys told "Try a sex toy for bonus".

Teenagers are also told "one of the best first steps you can take is connecting with your body by learning to masturbate" and sexual intimacy is "a powerful way to feel good and bond with another person, whether it's for a night or a lifetime".

While the *Let's Talk About It* book is unclassified and freely available in libraries across Australia it is so graphic coverage by News.com.au begins by telling viewers "Warning. The following images and/or content may be disturbing to some viewers. Viewer discretion is strongly advised".

As I've previously written in *The Daily Telegraph*, a third example of how children and teenagers are presented with what many parents would see as a one-sided and pornographic view of sexuality and gender is the inyourskin program.

The program's Instagram account tells students virginity is a myth guilty of perpetuating a heteronormative, binary concept based on "female sexual purity" and instead of being God given and a biological reality "sexuality has infinite possibilities".

Girls suffering gender dysphoria wanting to be boys are told chest binding is a good thing as it "can positively impact a person's health". Much like the neo-Marxist inspired Safe

Schools gender fluidity program inyourskin also champions LGBTIQA+ ideology.

The program celebrates Intersex Awareness Day, Transgender Awareness Week and Pansexual Pride Day with students told not to use pronouns like he or she. Students are also told "Everyone's sexual values are unique and it is not the place of others to dictate someone else's sexual values". So much for parental control.

While societies change and what is considered acceptable and not acceptable evolves over time there's no doubt, as argued by the Italian cultural critic Augusto Del Noce, Western societies like Australia have undergone a sexual revolution.

In the span of one generation, beginning with the sexual revolution of the late 1960s and early 1970's involving free love and the birth control pill, sexual mores and habits have been radically transformed.

No-where is this transformation more obvious than with what children and teenagers are told about sex, gender and sexuality. Primary age children are taught boys can be girls and girls can be boys and they have the power to self-identify anywhere on the LGBTIQA+ spectrum.

Sexual intimacy is no longer seen as special or reserved for a long tern relationship instead, as suggested by the *Let's Talk About It* book, a one-night stand is perfectly acceptable. Sex is no longer sacred or special but, instead, treated as an easily tradeable commodity.

Instead of learning the importance of restraint and not succumbing to immediate gratification students are told the guiding principle is self-pleasure and doing whatever is the most physically satisfying.

Also ignored is the need to respect the innocence and vulnerability of childhood and the reality many teenagers don't have the emotional or intellectual maturity to cope with a permissive, all things go attitude to sex and sexuality.

Parents are their children's primary guardians and authors, book publishers, schools and libraries should realise they also have a duty of care. While sex education is important it is vital that it is age appropriate, morally and ethically sound and not just based on the narcissistic belief if it feels good, do it.

Our schools are failing: this is why

Spectator Flat White, 4 August 2023

The news earlier this year Chairman Dan's government will use Victorian schools to promote a Yes case to the Voice should not surprise. Neither should it surprise in so many schools across Australia students, instead of saluting the flag and taking the oath of allegiance, are told to memorise the 'Uluru Statement from the Heart'.

There is nothing new or unusual about schools being used as vehicles to indoctrinate students with neo-Marxist inspired cultural-left ideology. It's been happening over the last 30 to 40 years. As I wrote in *Why our schools are failing* (2004), instead of viewing education as something objective and impartial, Australian schools have been pressured to adopt "an ideologically driven approach that defines education as an instrument to radically change society and turn students into politically correct, new-age warriors".

While the expression the long march through the institutions has become clichéd it does not alter the fact the phrase, attributed to the German student radical Rudi Dutschke and before him to the Italian Marxist Antonio Gramsci, very much describes what has occurred in education since the late 1970s.

At a Fabian Society meeting held in Melbourne in 1983 Joan Kirner, who later became Victoria's Minister for Education and then Premier, argued education had to be reshaped as "part of the socialist struggle for equality, participation and social change, rather than an instrument of the capitalist system". In the same speech Kirner argued schools must be used as "a catalyst for system change rather than the legitimization of system maintenance".

Kirner's socialist beliefs explain her mantra of equality of outcomes instead of equality of opportunity and her campaign to replace the then Higher School Certificate with the Victorian Certificate of Education. Given its academic focus and competitive end-of-year examinations where students are ranked in terms of performance Kirner argued the HSC unfairly favoured privileged students attending elite, wealthy non-government schools.

Not surprisingly, given its neo-Marxist leanings, the Australian Education Union (previously named the Australian Teachers Federation) over the last 40 years and similar to Joan Kirner argues Australian society is riven with inequality and injustice and teachers, in the words of a teacher training resource popular at the time, must decide whose side they are on.

The union's 1985 curriculum policy paper condemns Australian society for its "pronounced inequality in the distribution of social, economic, cultural and political resources and power between social groups, which restricts the life development of many". Teachers are also told the purpose of education and their role is to reveal to students "The role of the economy, the sexual division of labour, the dominant culture and the education system in reproducing inequality".

In order to improve equity and overcome disadvantage the Australian Education Union has consistently argued against Year 12 certificates, standardised tests like the National Assessment Program Literacy and Numeracy (NAPLAN) and what is described as the competitive, academic curriculum; a curriculum guilty of reinforcing capitalist hierarchies and disadvantaging at-risk, low socio-economic status (SES) students. The Union's 1998 curriculum policy paper states:

> *Reliance on competition is a primary cause of inequalities of educational outcome because students from certain social groups are advantaged by competitive selection methods. Competitive selection also sets students against each other rather than encouraging co-operative learning methods.*

Once again, the primary targets are Catholic and Independent schools that generally, with the exception of selective government schools like Melbourne High and Sydney's James Ruse Agricultural High School, achieve the strongest academic results as measured by the Year 12 Australian Tertiary Admission Rank (ATAR).

Other examples illustrating the AEU's cultural-left ideology and opposition to the belief education should be impartial and unbiased include denouncing the Howard government's involvement in the Iraqi war and suggesting students are entitled to strike in protest; arguing it's OK for students to wag school to attend climate change demonstrations; telling teachers they must embrace a neo-Marxist inspired LGBTIQA+ agenda and arguing non-government schools should not be funded.

Given the AEU's history of cultural-left activism it should not surprise the teacher union is a strong supporter of the Indigenous Voice to parliament. In its submission to the Indigenous Voice Co-Design process the union argues "The AEU strongly supports The Uluru Statement and Voice. Treaty. Truth. Specifically, the AEU wishes to emphasise the importance of Truth-telling in schools through and in the curriculum and in the Australian Professional Standards for Teachers".

As I detail in the chapter on school education in *Cancel Culture and the Left's Long March* subject associations like the Australian Association for the Teachers of English (AATE) have also been instrumental in radically reshaping the curriculum and what happens in the classroom. Similar to the AEU, the AATE also opposes standardised tests like NAPLAN on the basis, in relation to literacy, such tests stifle creativity by privileging correct grammar, spelling and punctuation and standardised English instead of the language students bring to the classroom.

Drawing on the work of the Brazilian Marxist educator Paulo Freire, who toured Australia in 1974, and the concept of critical literacy the AATE argues the purpose of teaching English is to liberate and empower students by enabling them to critique texts and to discover how language is employed to reinforce what Louis Althusser terms capitalist society's ideological state apparatus.

In an editorial in the 2004 edition of *English in Australia* published by the AATE Wayne Sawyer argues the re-election of the Howard led government demonstrated teachers had failed to properly teach critical literacy and, as a result, they had to redouble their efforts as so many young people had voted for the wrong party.

Critical literacy and a rainbow alliance of cultural-left theories including postmodernism, deconstructionism and radical feminist, gender and post-colonial theories have also had a profound impact on how literature is taught in the English classroom. The AATE condemns the concept of a literary canon involving those enduring works that are well crafted and have something profound to say about the human condition. Instead of acknowledging the moral, emotional and aesthetic value of literature students are made to deconstruct texts in terms of power relationships and how the voices of marginalised groups, including women, people of colour and LGBTIQA+ people, are ignored and silenced.

Two further examples of the way English teaching has been radically redefined are Volume 53, No 2, 2018 edition of *English in Australia* and a recent state conference organised by the Victorian Association for the Teaching of English (VATE). The edition of *English in Australia* tells teachers, as a result of the plebiscite to approve same-sex marriage being successful, English teachers must forsake literature perpetuating the "normalisation of heterosexuality" and cis-gendered relationships.

Instead, teachers are told to choose literature celebrating and normalising LGBTIQA+ relationships on the basis, as there are some in the community opposed to same-sex marriage, teachers should "make visible positive representations of diverse genders and sexualities. The inclusion of such characters in queer literature for young people makes it possible for such identities to be visible inside the school gates, in school libraries and in classrooms". Ignored are the beliefs of the nearly 40% of Australians who voted against same-sex marriage.

The second example of the English classroom being used to indoctrinate students is the 2022 VATE state conference where, as detailed by Mark Lopez in the January/February 2023 edition of *Quadrant*, teachers were told to ensure students are presented with a positive view about the Indigenous Voice to parliament. While the public might expect a conference of English teachers to focus on discussing the place of literacy and literature in the classroom Lopez, who attended the conference, writes "The real agenda of the conference was to mobilise English teachers to act as agents of left-wing social change to shape the minds of their students…".

The Australian Curriculum Studies Association (ACSA) is a peak professional body involving academics responsible for teacher training and its publication *Going Public: Education policy and public education in Australia* (1998), one again, illustrates how successful the cultural-left has been in taking control of education and seeking to enforce its ideology on schools. The book's editor describes it as "an unashamedly partisan book" and a "call to arms" as a result of what is seen as a conservative, neo-liberal agenda imposed by the then Liberal/National Government led by John Howard.

The book's conclusion argues any daring to question multiculturalism, the need for reconciliation or the ever-increasing cost of social welfare must be condemned for promoting "deep-seated prejudices, hatreds and fears that obviously lurk beneath the cosmopolitan veneer of Australian society".

In one chapter the authors, well known academics involved in teacher training, argue there is no literacy crisis and the Howard government, with the help of *The Australian* newspaper's "alarmist and negative reporting", manufactured the literacy crisis "to undermine the legitimacy of public belief in state schooling and, at the same time, to deflect attention away from material problems such as youth poverty and unemployment".

Drawing on neo-Marxist inspired critical theory and the works of Paulo Freire the authors argue, instead of concerns about poor literacy being genuine, government intervention is "motivated by a concern on the part of dominant cultural groups to organise and regulate the lives and learning of the disadvantaged and subaltern groups".

In 2006 ACSA organised a national forum involving all of Australia's left-leaning, progressive education establishment (what the UK education minister Michael Gove describes as the Blob), including professional bodies like the AATE and the AEU as well as state and territory education department representatives, to address the question of how best to achieve "excellence and equity in student learning outcomes". Once again, concerns expressed at the time regarding falling standards and a dumbed down curriculum were described by one speaker as a "conservative backlash" while another described it as "a concerted media attack".

A third speaker, after also questioning the legitimacy of complaints about falling standards, argued education in Australia was moving to a segregated system of schools with some students destined to receive "a basic education" while other more privileged students were granted a "broad, liberal education".

As to why education in Australia is dominated by cultural-left, politically correct ideology one needs to examine the impact of cultural Marxism and the rainbow alliance or radical theories that have impacted on the academy and teacher training beginning with the Frankfurt School established in Germany in the early 1920s.

Drawing on Antonio Gramsci's concept of capitalist hegemony, instead of focusing on the modes and means of production, activists argue the most effective way to overthrow the status quo and achieve the socialist utopia is to infiltrate and take control of society's institutions including universities, schools, the media, family and the church.

As noted by Michael Gove in *Celsius 7/7*, "The thinkers of the Frankfurt School revived Marxism as primarily a cultural rather than an economic movement. In place of anger against traditional capitalism, scorn was directed at the reining value systems of the West". What Louise Althusser would later describe as the ideological state apparatus explains why, even though citizens are oppressed and disadvantaged, such is the power of capitalist conditioning and thought control they mistakenly believe all is well.

The cultural-left's domination of education can also be explained by the cultural revolution of the late 1960s and early 1970s, a time of student riots at the Sorbonne, anti-Vietnam demonstrations, Woodstock and the youth counter-culture movement. Gove makes the point many of those students radicalised at university during the cultural revolution went on to take up positions in universities, schools, the media and political parties and organisations where they embarked on a radical push to change society.

The late 60s and early 70s also saw the emergence of a rainbow alliance of theories including deconstructionism, postmodernism and extreme feminist, gender and post-colonial theories. While not always in agreement, what all hold in common is a radical critique of capitalist society and Western civilisation and the belief universities and schools are a primary target to achieve change.

Roger Scruton in *Culture Counts* describes this rainbow alliance as enforcing a "culture of repudiation" responsible for spawning:

> ... *a massive literature of cultural subversion throughout the post-war period, from Foucault's analysis of knowledge as the ideology of power to Richard Rorty's truth-denying pragmatism, and from Barthes's structuralist debunking of the classics to the 'deconstructive virus' released into the academic air by Jacques Derrida.*

Drawing largely on cultural Marxism and the emergence of theory during the early to mid-70s what became known as the new sociology of education movement began to replace the more liberal view of education dedicated to what TS Eliot describes as "the pursuit of truth, and in so far as men are capable of it, the attainment of wisdom".

How schools and the curriculum are organised and structured, for example, instead of being inherently worthwhile and beneficial are seen as social constructs designed to reinforce the status quo and favour the sons and daughters of capitalist elites. More extreme advocates for change, such as America's Samuel Bowles and Herbert Gintis, argue if capitalism is to be overthrown education has to be reimagined as a critical part of the "revolutionary, democratic socialist movement".

The Australian Education Union's attack on the traditional, academic curriculum, where competition and meritocracy prevail, draws heavily on the new sociology of education as does its argument Catholic and Independent schools do not deserve government funding. Underlying the Gonski review of school funding and the argument investing additional billions will improve standards and overcome disadvantage is also the belief society is structured hierarchically where wealthy, privileged students are guaranteed success while working class, migrant and indigenous students are always destined to underachieve.

Whether academics at the University of Sydney opposing the establishment of a Centre for Western Civilisation, schools teaching the neo-Marxist inspired Safe Schools gender fluidity program, students being encouraged to wag school and strike to stop global warming or the way history enforces a black armband view, the reality is the cultural-left's long march has succeeded beyond expectations.

The barbarians are no longer at the gate, they have taken the citadel. Of even greater concern, with very few exceptions, is that successive commonwealth liberal governments and education minsters including Julie Bishop, Christopher Pyne, Dan Tehan and Alan Tudge vacated the field and did nothing to engage in what John Howard terms the battle of ideas.

While much of the public commentary and political debate surrounding school education focuses on funding issues, complaints about falling standards and the most effective way to ensure teacher quality, as important is the way the cultural-left dominates what is taught and what happens in the classroom. Instead of being impartial and balanced on issues like global warming, the arrival of the First Fleet and European settlement, the benefits of Western civilisation and what constitutes human sexuality, students are given a jaundiced and one-sided view.

How the classroom is structured and how students are assessed has also fallen victim to progressive, new-age ideology. Instead of summative assessment, where 4/10 means fail, teachers rely of formative, diagnostic assessment based on developmental continuums making it impossible to rank students in terms of performance or to measure progress against year level objective standards. Student self-esteem and self-agency prevail where teachers are facilitators and guides by the side while students are described as knowledge navigators and digital natives.

Even though research proves memorisation and rote learning are vital in order to ensure automaticity (the ability to quickly recall facts, dates, events and information stored in one's long term memory) schools have long condemned such practices as making students mindlessly parrot what has been taught.

When Ronald Reagan was President a report titled *A Nation at Risk: The Imperative for Educational Reform* concluded:

> ... *the educational foundations of our society are presently being eroded by a rising tide of mediocrity that threatens our very future as a Nation and a People... If an unfriendly foreign power had attempted to impose on America the mediocre educational performance that exists today, we might well have viewed it as an act of war.*

The American report's conclusion equally applies to Australia's education system.

Teacher training not the only answer for better outcomes

Daily Telegraph, 2 August 2023

There's no doubt beginning teachers need to be well trained and expert in what constitutes the most effective and engaging way to teach and how best to control the classroom. There's also no doubt too many teachers enter schools unprepared and too many leave the profession early.

Released by the Commonwealth Minister for Education Jason Clare the report into teacher training titled 'Strong Beginnings' seeks to remedy the problem by ensuring teacher training is based on sound research and made publicly accountable.

The report begins by repeating the clichés and jargon much loved by official reports. Teachers are told their job is to ensure students "master new skills and talents" in order to "constructively find solutions" in what is described as a "complex, fast-changing multicultural society".

Ignored is the need to ensure beginning teachers appreciate their role in providing students with an intellectually rigorous education that is morally and spiritually enriching and emotionally grounded.

Nowhere in the teacher training report is there any recognition equally as important as schools and teachers contributing to the nation's "competitiveness, economic strength and prosperity" is the need to promote cultural literacy and societal stability and cohesion.

One of the most debilitating aspects of education is the way governments and bureaucracies enforce an inflexible one size-fits-all, top down approach. The pendulum swings between extremes instead of recognising there is no magic bullet that meets every situation.

Since the late 1960s and early 1970s teacher training has embraced progressive fads and innovations like open classrooms, inquiry based learning where content is secondary to process and where the student is centre stage instead of the teacher being an authority figure.

The current danger, given the report's recommendation forcing teacher training institutions to replace the more new-age approach with one that is highly structured and inflexible, is that beginning teachers' educational toolkit, once again, will be one-dimensional and limited.

Experienced teachers know when it comes to handling a class and ensuring students are engaged and learning there is no one approach suited to every occasion or every student. What happens early in the week is often very different to what is needed on Friday afternoon.

While mandating explicit teaching where the teacher is in control is long overdue and learning how to read using a phonics and phonemic awareness model is commendable teachers need to master a variety of teaching strategies and practices.

Reading the 14 recommendations in the report it's obvious the solution proposed by the expert panel involves a highly regulated, bureaucratic regime guaranteed to promote a time consuming check list mentality.

Similar to the Australian Institute for Teaching and School Leadership that stipulates hundreds of indicators detailing what constitutes graduate, proficient, highly accomplished and lead teachers the teacher training report imposes a highly regulated list of demands.

The teacher training report is also flawed as it fails to take a holistic approach to the challenge of raising standards and ensuring students leave school with an enriching, rigorous and worthwhile educational experience.

While teacher training is important even more important is the fact the national curriculum, despite numerous reviews and submissions, is still overcrowded, dumbed down and impossible to teach.

The national curriculum should be cut back to 60% of the school week and the focus should be on what is essential instead of pressuring teachers to include Woke issues like climate change, indigenous history, gender fluidity and wellness.

One of the reasons teaching has such a high burn out rate and why so many are leaving the profession early is because the current assessment and reporting system is overly complicated and time consuming.

Teachers are expected to monitor and evaluate every student in every class and every lesson using formative assessment. Instead of summative assessment involving tests and marks out of 10 formative assessment is time consuming and onerous as teachers are made to write lengthy descriptive reports – often pages long.

Parents also must take responsibility for making teachers' work more challenging and difficult as too many children go to school without being taught to respect authority, do as their told and work hard to succeed.

What politicians like Labor's Jason Clare fail to realise is teaching and how best to raise standards and improve outcomes is a complex and difficult task where numerous factors are inter-related.

Focusing on one factor like teacher training is guaranteed to be ineffective. It is also vital to free schools from the provider capture imposed by governments, bureaucracies and teacher unions like the NSW Teachers Federation.

As with charter schools in America and free schools in Britain autonomy and flexibility is needed giving schools greater control in areas like staffing, school ethos and curriculum focus.

Gender ideology is front and centre in our schools

Daily Telegraph, 27 June 2023

The inyourskin Relationships and Sexuality Education program is the most recent example proving how radical gender and sexuality ideology dominates the nation's schools. Parents need to realise their children are being indoctrinated with bizarre and unnatural beliefs about what it means to be male or female.

Instead of gender and sexuality being biologically determined and God given, in pre-schools and primary and secondary schools children and teenagers are being taught gender and sexuality are fluid and dynamic social constructs and they can identify any-where on the LGBTIQA+ spectrum.

The inyourskin program offers a comprehensive relationships and sexuality education to a range of clients including government and non-government schools, state and territory education departments and professional bodies including the Association of Heads of Independent Schools of Australia.

Under the heading of 'Student Workshops' topics covered include exploring the "general experience of queer students (and) the harmful impact of gender binary language" and "taking a gender transformative approach... to develop a healthy and realistic sense of the 'other'".

While the program offers a range of less controversial services and workshops dealing with sexual violence, consent and the dangers of intoxication, the materials showcased on the inyourskin Instagram account illustrate how Woke and controversial the program is.

Under the heading 'What is the Sexuality Spectrum?' students are told sexuality has "infinite possibilities" and that everyone's "sexual identities and orientations are complex and unique". When describing pansexuality, students are told an individual's gender need not be restricted by "biological sex, gender or gender identity".

In this fluid and dynamic world of Woke gender ideology children and teenagers are told the possibilities are limitless as they have the right to choose between whether they are "non-binary, genderqueer, a Sistergirl or Brotherboy, genderfluid".

When it comes to the question of virginity those responsible for the inyourskin material also adopt a very progressive, new-age approach. Under the heading 'Virginity is a harmful social construct' students are told "virginity is not something that can be defined" and the concept of virginity "perpetrates a heteronormative context" where the assumption is "gender is binary".

Other examples of materials offered to schools include, 'What is ethical porn?', 'International safe abortion day' and 'What is binding?' where students are told "Binding is a process of flattening the chest" and "Binding can positively impact on a person's mental health".

If programs and resources produced by the inyourskin were an isolated example of what is happening in schools then matters would not be as distressing. If such programs were balanced, objective and based on common sense and morally sound they might be of some benefit.

The reality, though, is since the gender fluidity Safe Schools program was developed in 2010 radical gender and sexuality activists have targeted schools and students in their campaign to overturn the nuclear family and indoctrinate students with their destructive ideology.

The national professional body for government schoolteachers, the Australian Education Union, argues the school curriculum must acknowledge and celebrate those identifying as LGBTIQA+ on the basis societies like Australia are guilty of heteronormativity, cis-genderism and homophobia/transphobia.

The Australian Association for the Teaching of English tells classroom teachers fairy tales like *Cinderella* and *Sleeping Beauty*, plus Shakespeare's *Romeo and Juliet* and Jane Austen's *Pride and Prejudice*, are also guilty as they normalise the love between a woman and a man.

It's common for primary and secondary classrooms to display rainbow flags, to tell students to use gender neutral pronouns like 'they' and 'zie' and to celebrate Pride month and IDAHOBIT Day.

Some schools go to the extent of inviting drag queens into the classroom, having non-gendered uniforms and allowing students who self-identify differently to their birth sex to use the toilets and changing rooms they feel best suits their new identity.

Ignored in the rush to overturn biology and common sense – men have penises while women have vaginas and can give birth and breast feed babies – is how wrong it is to indoctrinate young and vulnerable children and teenagers with controversial views about gender and sexuality.

Misgivings and concerns about the medical and ethical dangers in encouraging children and teenagers to deny their biological gender and sex explains why medical experts and doctors in the UK and Europe are warning that the rush to embrace radical gender theory must be stopped.

It is also wrong to deny the right parents have as their children's primary care givers and moral guardians to be responsible for their children's education regarding gender and sexuality. It's time for Australian politicians to follow the example of Ron DeSantis in Florida and support parents in their battle to assert their rights and protect their children.

Enduring truths and neglected lessons

Quadrant, 22 June 2023

Much of the debate surrounding schools and education centres on falling standards, teacher quality, school funding and what constitutes the most worthwhile curriculum and effective pedagogy.

While such matters are important, more significant is the question, what constitutes the purpose of education? Given the rise of AI and Chatbots and the fear humans will soon be replaced by computers the question is even more urgent.

Drawing on cultural-Marxism and critical theory one answer is to use education as an instrument to overthrow what is seen as an inherently unjust and oppressive Western, capitalist society. Education is about empowerment and liberation.

Students are taught about the dangers of global warming, that gender and sexuality are fluid and limitless and it is wrong to be sexist, racist or homophobic/transphobic. The purpose of education is to bring about change.

In its most extreme, as a result of post-colonial theory and postmodernism, students are presented with a dark view of Western civilisation and Australia's development as a nation since the arrival of the First Fleet in 1788.

When Julia Gillard was education minister she described herself as the minister for productivity. The focus is a utilitarian one where the purpose of education is to strengthen the economy and to ensure the nation has a highly skilled, globally competitive workforce.

Associated with using schools to increase productivity is ensuring students are prepared for the uncertain, ever-changing world of the 21ˢᵗ century. Knowledge is secondary to teaching generic competencies and skills like creativity, working in teams, critical thinking and embracing diversity and difference.

Ensuring education, especially in primary schools, is child-centred represents yet another approach to defining the purpose of education. Rebadged as personalised learning and student agency the belief learning only comes alive when it embraces the world of the child.

While each of the above models are distinctive what they hold in common is the failure to address the essential role education plays in enculturation. If societies are to survive and prosper and if individuals are to find meaning and purpose each succeeding generation needs to be initiated into the broader culture.

The American academic Christopher J Lucas makes the point culture is learned and argues "The culture of a society must be internalised by each generation. Education, informal and formal, unconscious and conscious, is a means for the preservation of culture".

Edmund Burke also stresses the need for continuity when he describes the relationship between citizens and a civil society as a partnership "not only between those who are living, but between those who are living, those who are dead, and those who are yet to be born".

At a time when cultural relativism prevails it is vital to realise not all cultures are the same and, in relation to Australia, our institutions, language, religion, music, literature and the arts have grown out of Western civilisation.

The school curriculum must acknowledge such a reality and, in the same way the national curriculum calls on schools to teach indigenous history, spirituality and culture, it stands to reason students have the right to be introduced to that corpus of knowledge, understanding and skills beginning with the ancient Greeks and evolving over thousands of years.

Such an education, what Saint John Henry Newman describes as a liberal education, is neither practical and utilitarian nor limited to the world of the child. A liberal education is grounded in the established disciplines and, unlike cultural-left politically correct ideology, is impartial and disinterested.

The ideal is to enable students to be critically aware, independent thinkers and to be culturally literate, morally grounded and spiritually enriched. Such an education also cultivates virtues such as courage, temperateness, justice and good sense as well as a commitment to social justice and the common good.

While often condemned as backward looking and ossified a liberal education also embraces change. As noted by Matthew Arnold, the need is to turn "a stream of fresh and free thought upon our stock notions and habits".

A liberal education also introduces students to a conversation that deals with eternal truths that have existed since sentient humans first walked the earth. Existential questions about the meaning of life, what constitutes fulfilment and happiness and what happens after death are ever present.

At a time when the education debate centres on funding, teacher quality, pedagogy and falling standards and the commonwealth education minister Jason Clare has commissioned yet more inquires it's vital to return to first principles.

It's also timely to reaffirm the belief that no amount of AI and Chatbots can ever replace the patrimony represented by Western civilisation's enduring cultural heritage.

Chalk and Cheese: Then and Now

Quadrant Online, 25 May 2023

In chapter one of CS Lewis' *The Abolition of Man*, published in 1944, Lewis criticises the way education, instead of teaching students to discriminate between what is true and false and what is good and bad, conditions them to rely on emotions and a subjective view of how individuals relate to one another and perceive and understand the world.

In opposition, drawing on Platonic, Aristotelian, Stoic, Christian and Oriental teachings (what he describes as the Tao), Lewis writes "… what is common to them all is something we cannot neglect. It is the doctrine of objective value, the belief that certain attitudes are really true, and others are really false, to the kind of thing the universe is and the kind of things we are".

Lewis goes on to suggest, for those immersed in the Tao, calling children delightful and old men venerable is not "to record a psychological fact about our own parental or filial emotions at the moment, but to recognise a quality which *demands* a certain response from us whether we make it or not".

Central to Lewis' argument is that children must be taught to appreciate the true nature of things as opposed to the progressive, romanticised view that children grow naturally to discernment and knowledge (now rebadged as self-agency and personalised learning where teachers are guides by the side).

Lewis writes children "must be trained to feel pleasure, liking, disgust and hatred of those things which really are pleasant, likeable, disgusting and hateful". For teachers to do otherwise is to impoverish children with a barren, soulless and ego-centred education more akin to what he describes as "merely propaganda".

Pierre Ryckmans, in his 1996 Boyer Lectures, also stresses the danger of subjectivism. After recounting an episode where an academic attacks Chinese literati painting as bourgeois Ryckmans writes "From his perspective, value judgments were necessarily a form of cultural arrogance… a vain and subjective expression of social prejudice". Ryckmans goes on to argue, given the lack of objective values, universities are now dead, but nobody has noticed.

The way literature is taught in schools provides a striking example of how destructive and impoverished education has become. Since the mid-to-late 1960's the definition of literature has been exploded to include multi-media texts, graffiti, SMS texting, posters and a student's own writing.

No longer are students introduced to classic myths, fables, legends and fairy tales and those enduring works that have stood the test of time, have something profound and insightful to say about human nature and the circumambient universe and that are exemplary examples of their craft. As argued by British academic Terry Eagleton:

> *…there is no such thing as a literary work or tradition which is valuable in itself, regardless of what anyone might have said or come to say about it. 'Value' is a transitive term: it means whatever is valued by certain people in specific situations, according to particular criteria and in the light of given purposes.*

In addition to literature being reduced to social constructs students, even when they encounter what was once termed the literary canon, are taught to analyse such works in terms of neo-Marxist and postmodern inspired critical theory and critical literacy.

Instead of being appreciated for their moral, spiritual and aesthetic qualities the works of Chaucer, Donne, Shakespeare, Austen, Dickens, Yeats and Dostoyevsky are analysed and critiqued in terms of power relationships and how they enforce the hegemony of a Eurocentric, imperialist, heteronormative and exploitive, capitalist society.

Whereas studying literature once involved humility, patience and a willingness to accept one's own knowledge and understanding was, by necessity limited, students are now taught the author is dead, there are as many interpretations of a text as there are readers and that texts have no inherent value or meaning.

The Bible, instead of being the word of God, is simply yet another text among many that has to be analysed and deconstructed in terms of its time and place instead of expressing eternal truths about what constitutes good and evil and how best to find redemption and salvation.

Some years back an editorial in *The Australian* newspaper suggested "the act of imaginative empathy is a virtue to be encouraged". Atticus, Scout's father in *To Kill a Mockingbird,* says something similar when he says: "You never really understand a person until you consider things from his point of view, until you climb into his skin and walk around in it".

As William Blake understood, literature, at its best, allows the reader to cleanse the doors of perception and to enter an imaginative world to experience emotions and thoughts in a uniquely moving and intense way. Such an encounter involves what Coleridge terms "the willing suspension of disbelief". A gift denied by neo-Marxist inspired postmodern theory that puts Shakespeare's *King Lear* on the same level as an Ikea self-help manual and where students are forced to deconstruct literature in terms of power, victimhood and identity politics.

Background no reason for failing standards

Daily Telegraph, 28 April 2023

If any further evidence is needed as to why Australian students are going backwards in international maths, science and literacy tests and why so many lack resilience and the ability to overcome adversity look no further than the forthcoming webinar on education organised by the Australian Human Rights Commission.

While schools should be places where teachers teach and students are introduced to what the *Victorian Blackburn Report* describes as "our best validated knowledge and artistic achievements" the organisers ask, "Can we shake up the limiting notion that the primary task of schools is academic achievement".

Titled 'Reinventing schools to support learning and wellbeing for all' the organisers argue "now is the time to reinvigorate schools, to become places that focus on the whole child's health, wellbeing and learning".

In the trite and meaningless edu-speak characteristic of what now passes as education the organisers go on to ask, "How can we make schools places to amplify children's physical and mental wellbeing (and) give them the opportunity to thrive and make them life-long learners".

Welcome to schools of the 21st century; a time of holistic learning when teachers act as social workers, psychologists and wellness experts instead of masters of their subject and where learning is reduced to emotional therapy.

Ignored is parents are their children's primary care givers responsible for their emotional and mental wellbeing. Also ignored, and contrary to the prevailing cosmic karma zeitgeist, is schools are not centres of counselling and psychotherapy and teachers are not health professionals.

Closely linked to the belief education, instead of promoting academic achievement, must be warm, fuzzy and stress free is the idea learning mustn't be onerous and challenging. Failing students is bad for their self-esteem and pressuring them to work hard to succeed creates unfair expectations.

No wonder, according to the OECD's 2023 Australian education profile, since the year 2000 "Australia has experienced persistently declining student outcomes across PISA cycles in the three main subjects, with an increase in the share of low-performing students".

Despite the additional billions invested and the plethora of government innovations including the national curriculum and national teaching standards designed to improve students' performance and make schools more effective results have only gone backwards.

Proven by London's Michaela Community School founded by Katherine Birbalsingh, who recently visited Australia, and the 'No Excuses' schools in America there is an alternative to Australia's feel-good, dumbed down education system.

Such has been the success of the school Birbalsingh established, based on strong academic standards and classroom disciple, the United Kingdom's Ofsted school inspectors rate the school as outstanding with higher than average GCSE results.

The American No Excuses schools are also popular, especially in disadvantaged inner urban areas, and unlike most Australian schools enforce a strict discipline policy and challenging standards on the basis high expectations breed confidence and success.

The No Excuses educational philosophy also involves clear rules, strong parental involvement and supportive school communities. Unlike Australian classrooms, among the most disruptive with badly behaved students across the OECD, teachers in No Excuses schools can focus all their energy on teaching.

While the wellness, kumbaya movement helps to explain why academic standards are going backwards, equally as damaging is the cultural-left's belief success depends on a student's home background. Students from working class and migrant communities, compared to those from more affluent families, are always disadvantaged.

The rationale behind the multi-billion dollar Gonski school funding model, for example, is based on the belief a student's home background as measured by parents' education, occupational class and income is the main source of inequality. The assumption is if schools are given more money standards will automatically improve.

The commonwealth minister for education, Jason Clare, when announcing yet another series of costly, bureaucratic and ineffective government enquiries into falling standards, always cites home background as the main cause of disadvantage.

The only problem is home background is not the major issue. As noted by an analysis of the 2018 PISA results, "Australia has comparatively high levels of academic inclusiveness in schools, with socio-economic status having a less profound influence on reading performance than on average across the OECD".

A recent research article titled *Socioeconomic status (SES): A Failing but Enduring Paradigm* by Australian academic Gary Marks provides additional evidence home background has only a minor influence of students' academic ability.

Marks describes the SES paradigm as spurious and instead argues more important factors than postcode and parents' occupation and wealth are what students have inherited from their parents in terms of ability and motivation, plus curriculum rigour, teacher quality and a disciplined school environment based on high expectations.

We need to restore the sense of optimism in our kids

Daily Telegraph, 21 April 2023

There's no doubt today's children and teenagers lack the resilience and ability to overcome adversity compared to generations past. Evidence includes the dramatic increase in prescribing drugs to treat anxiety and depression. An increase from 13,000 in 2012 to 29,228 in 2022 according to the Pharmaceutical Benefits Scheme.

Add the fact it's now common for primary and secondary schools to have special wellness programs as part of the school curriculum and the number of teachers complaining about having to be counsellors and social workers it's obvious there is a problem.

While the lockdowns and school closures as a result of the Covid-19 pandemic are a factor contributing to stress and anxiety, plus the high rates of cyber bullying and sexting, equally as significant is the way children are mollycoddled and protected by their parents.

Gone are the days when kids were free range, riding bikes without helmets, bouncing on trampolines without safety nets and playing British Bulldog and stacks on the mill. Instead of taking risks and experiencing pain children are wrapped in cotton wool and protected.

Parents letting their children spend hours and hours every day in front of screens living in a virtual world or shutting themselves in their bedrooms conversing with friends on mobile phones does nothing to prepare them for life's challenges in what is a difficult world.

Driving children to school, instead of making them walk, letting them ride a bike or take public transport, in addition to clogging up the roads during the early morning and late afternoon rush, breeds dependence.

Schools are also to blame for forcing on students a negative, depressing and unsettling politically correct agenda that destroys any sense of optimism and confidence about the future. Students are told the world is facing a cataclysmic end where all will be lost because of climate change.

Students are also taught Australian society is inherently racist and oppressive where Indigenous Australians are victims of white supremacism and current generations of young people and their parents are guilty of events that occurred hundreds of years ago.

Society is also inherently sexist, homophobic and transphobic and beginning in primary school children, especially boys, are told they are complicit in reinforcing heteronormative, binary attitudes instead of embracing diversity and difference.

No wonder rates of anxiety and depression are increasing as students are fed a steady diet of negativity where all is guilt, gloom and doom. There is an alternative. Instead of always focusing on the negative it's time to give young people a sense of confidence and hope.

It's vital to let children be children giving them the time and space to enjoy the innocence of childhood. Allowing adults to impose their bleak, joyless ideology on minors might give them a warm feeling of moral superiority, but it does nothing to instil optimism.

Also important are literary classics like *The Iliad* and *The Odyssey* and heroic figures like Queen Boadicea who fought the Romans and Beowulf who defeated the Grendel as they teach children the importance of courage and bravery.

As argued by the American academic Joseph Campbell and the psychologist Bruno Bettelheim myths, fables and legends are vital in giving children a sense of resilience and the ability to overcome fear and adversity.

Instead of making young people feel guilty about being Australian schools should teach them how fortunate they are to live in a society, compared to Russia, China, Iran, Cuba and Venezuela, where liberties and freedoms are protected.

While there is inequality and hardship, proven by the millions of migrants who have arrived since the end of the 11 World War, Australia is a beacon of stability and security where with hard work, effort and ability it is possible to achieve prosperity and success.

While Woke activists committed to neo-Marxist inspired, post-colonial theory condemn Western civilisation as racist and guilty of imperialism and colonialism it's also time to teach young people the unique strengths and benefits of Australia as an outpost of Western culture.

The nation's political and legal systems based on popular sovereignty and all being equal before the law ensure all have the freedom to go about their lives without undue government interference and control.

Christianity, as Australia's major religion, also needs to be acknowledged and appreciated as concepts like love thy neighbour as thyself, do good instead of evil and commit to social justice and help those less advantaged are based on Christ's teachings and the New Testament.

The world today's students will inherit is a complex, difficult and challenging one compared to days past. As such, it's even more important to focus on optimism, resilience and nation building.

Religious freedom is so important for schools

Daily Telegraph, 10 March 2023

There's no doubt the Australian Law Reform Commission's review of faith-based schools and the right to operate and manage themselves according to their religious beliefs and convictions represents yet another attack on religious freedom.

At the moment, according to commonwealth law, when it comes to staffing and enrolments religious schools are allowed to discriminate "in order to avoid injury to the religious susceptibilities of adherents of that religion or creed" and if discrimination occurs "in good faith".

As argued by Australia's Catholic Bishops, "It is a reasonable expectation by religious organisations that those who choose to work in them do not compromise or 'injure' by word or action those religious and moral principles from which the agencies derive their foundational beliefs".

Religious freedom is also guaranteed by the *Universal Declaration of Human Rights* that states "Everyone has the right to freedom of thought, conscience and religion", including the "freedom, either alone or in community with others and in public or private, to manifest his religion or belief in teaching, practice, worship and observance".

Being able to discriminate makes sense. In the same way women's gyms can say no to men and single-sex schools are allowed to exist, it's only right religious schools have the freedom to organise and manage themselves according to the religious teachings they are committed to uphold.

When it comes to sexuality and gender, if Christian schools are to remain true to the Bible when it states "male and female He created them", it's wrong to force schools to employ an activist LGBTIQ+ teacher who disagrees with and undermines the school's position.

The closure of the transgender Tavistock Clinic in England and the increasing number of European countries warning about the dangers of puberty blockers and irreversible surgery also suggests faith-based schools should not be coerced into embracing radical gender theory.

The likelihood of this happening is significant given the ALRC's proposal staff employed in religious schools must be free to express "their own sex, sexual orientation, gender identity, marital and relationship status or pregnancy in connection with work or in private life".

Even worse, if the ALRC's proposal is accepted that schools have to conform to the government's curriculum about sex and sexual orientation, is schools could be made to teach programs like the neo-Marxist inspired Safe Schools gender fluidity program that contradicts religious beliefs.

Safe Schools teaches boys can be girls and girls can be boys and, contrary to religious teachings and human biology, they have the freedom to decide where they fit on the LGBTIQ+ spectrum.

Forcing faith-based schools to act against their religious beliefs is especially wrong given parents, who are their children's primary guardians, have the right to expect whatever school they choose supports their beliefs, values and morals.

The international *Convention against Discrimination in Education* upholds parents' rights when it states they have the right to choose a school where the "religious and moral education of the children (is) in conformity with their own convictions".

Numerous surveys show one of the reasons enrolments in Catholic, Independent and Christian schools are outstripping government schools, an increase of 16,4% compared to 1.9% over the last 5 years, is because parents want an education that provides a substantial, well-grounded moral compass for their children.

That parents must be allowed to choose faith-based schools that have the freedom to mirror their morals and beliefs is especially important given government schools are secular and not allowed to evangelise when it comes to religion.

One of the concessions to religious freedom granted by the ALRC is the right faith-based schools have to discriminate in relation to staff directly responsible for teaching religious doctrine or belief. But even here, the right to protect religious freedom is illusory.

The ALRC proposes any LGBTIQ+ staff asked to teach religious education must have the right to teach "alternative viewpoints", even if they contradict the school's religious beliefs. There is also the issue ignored by the ALRC's consultation paper that all staff members are responsible to support a school's religious ethos.

Underpinning the ALRC's consultation paper is the belief individual rights are paramount and religious teachings and beliefs are secondary. Ignored is every school and organisation, secular or faith-based, operates as a community where all those involved need to be committed and fully supportive.

This is especially the case for religious schools as such schools are established for the purpose of imbuing students with their unique moral and spiritual beliefs and virtues. If there are teachers, parents or students hostile or unwilling to conform to religious teachings the obvious answer is the government system.

Religious schools have the right to discriminate

The Age, 21 February 2023

Should religious schools and other education bodies have the right, as they now do, to discriminate when it comes to who they employ and who they enrol?

The overwhelming majority of non-government schools are faith-based and committed to teaching the tenets of their particular religion. Given their religious character the question arises as to what extent they should be free to manage themselves free of intervention.

At the request of Attorney-General Mark Dreyfus the Australian Law Reform Commission has released a consultation paper putting forward its proposals for how the federal government should address these questions with submissions closing on Friday.

Its findings could have direct consequences for the 2724 religious non-government schools across Australia plus the over 1.4 million students and their parents who make financial sacrifices when choosing such schools.

The Labor government is committed to enacting reforms to ensure students cannot be discriminated against on grounds of sexual orientation, gender identity, marital or relationship status, or pregnancy, with teachers protected from discrimination on the same grounds.

Religious schools would be allowed to give preference to prospective staff on religious grounds where the teaching, observance, or practise of religion is a part of their role and not otherwise discriminatory.

Groups like the Australian Education Union and the human rights group Equality Australia argue schools and other education bodies should no longer have control over staffing and student enrolments. They argue it's unfair and discriminatory.

Religious leaders from across Australia representing Catholic, Jewish, Islamic, Anglican, Presbyterian religions, the Australian Christian Lobby and the National Civic Council argue the opposite, saying faith-based schools must be allowed to act according to their religious tenets and beliefs.

Often forgotten or ignored in debates about human rights is there is no such thing as unlimited freedom to do whatever you want. Within a liberal, democratic society like Australia each person's rights are always balanced against the rights of others and the community in general.

When it comes to employment, for example, there are times when the right to be employed has to be balanced against the right of employers to ensure their employees support and don't undermine the organisation's charter, mission and values.

The Greens Party wouldn't want to employ a climate sceptic who wanted more coal mines, just as a refugee activist group would not want to employ someone who was racist and xenophobic or a feminist collective employ a sexist male who disliked women.

Any reasonable person would say no way to such scenarios. It's long been accepted there are times when it is OK to discriminate. One's person's freedom always has to be balanced against the beliefs and convictions of others.

It's only common sense to ask why someone with a strong commitment to a particular set of values would want to apply for a job in an organisation or workplace that holds different values. The right to balance freedoms and sometimes discriminate is especially true for religious schools.

Whether Christian, Islamic, Jewish or one of the many other faiths, the whole purpose of such schools is to teach the tenets of their religion and imbue students with their unique spiritual and moral teachings.

In an increasingly multicultural, multi-faith society like Australia it is vital all faith-based schools, regardless of their religious character, have the freedom to best reflect the needs and aspirations of their various communities.

The uniquely religious nature of faith-based schools must be protected. Students who attend Christian schools, based on a Cardus education survey, are more civic-minded than graduates of government schools as measured by involvement in political parties, professional associations, sporting and cultural groups.

The idea of removing the right religious schools currently have to discriminate over staffing and enrolments represents a fundamental attack on religious freedom.

Removing or seriously compromising such religious freedom also represents an attack on the right parents have to choose a school where the staff, the school's curriculum and the way the school is managed mirrors their religious beliefs and values.

Parents are their children's primary educators and moral guardians and they must be confident the religious schools they choose have the freedom to remain true to their faith.

The lesson some find difficult to absorb

Quadrant Online, 15 February 2023

With the start of the school year, it should not surprise the hoary debate about school funding is alive and well in the pages of the left-of-centre press. Julie Szego (The Age 2/2/23) argues non-government schools are overfunded, compared to needy government schools, and the imbalance must be redressed.

More extreme critics of Catholic and Independent schools go as far as arguing parents sending their children to non-government schools should not be financially supported by governments as only state schools deserve funding.

Jenna Price (SMH 31/1/23), based on a recent Four Corners one-sided episode attacking a number of Opus Dei linked schools in Sydney, argues "There is no better time to defund private schools than now".

Whereas government schools are described as "values-led", when it comes to non-government schools Price argues "If there are values, it is about keeping power in the hands of the wealthy and already powerful".

In its submission to the Gonski review of school funding established when Julia Gillard was the education minister the AEU argues, "we believe there is no pre-existing, pre-determined entitlement to public funding; i.e. there is no a priori justification for public funding of private schools".

More recently in a media release 20th January the AEU argues, "It's astonishing that 'record funding' continues to get headlines when teachers across the nation know that this funding has not gone to public schools but to the private sector".

According to 2019-2020 figures published on the ACARA website government schools receive $20,182 per student in recurrent funding from commonwealth, state and territory governments while non-government schools only receive $13,189.

At approximately 34 per cent of enrolments every student who attends a Catholic or Independent school, because they are not fully funded by governments, save taxpayers billions of dollars every year. One estimate by Independent Schools Australia puts that saving at $5.5 billion annually.

Parents sending their children to Catholic and Independent schools, in addition to paying non-government school fees, as taxpayers also contribute to the cost of financing state schools. Based on equity it's only fair such parents receive some government support.

When arguing non-government schools are over-funded it's important to understand the amount of government funding is adjusted by a school's capacity to contribute. More privileged schools receive far less than schools serving less affluent communities.

The reality is for every one wealthy, privileged non-government school like Geelong Grammar and Sydney's The King's School there are hundreds of non-government schools, especially Catholic parish schools, serving low to middle-class socio-economic status communities.

Often ignored in debates about funding is the right parents have to choose where their children go to school and what sort of education they receive. Parents have the right to ensure schools reflect their moral and ethical beliefs and values.

Unlike government schools, non-government schools are religious in nature, with the overwhelming majority being either Catholic schools or Independent schools affiliated with various religions ranging from Anglican to non-denominational and Islamic to Baptist. Given the secular nature of government schools where religion is not a significant part of what is taught plus the importance of religious freedom, it's only fair and just religious parents are not financially penalised as a result of school choice.

Underpinning the school funding debate is the belief socio-economic status is the prime determinant of educational outcomes and by cutting back funding to non-government schools and prioritising needy government schools more disadvantaged students will achieve success.

The evidence proves otherwise. The Director of Education and Skills at the OECD Andreas Schleicher in *PISA 2018 Insights and Instructions* argues "social disadvantage does not automatically lead to poor educational performance for students and schools".

The Australian academic Gary Marks in *Education Social Background and Cognitive Ability* argues socioeconomic background "is only moderately associated with educational outcomes". Based on the PISA international test results Marks puts the figure at 7-15 percent.

Research suggests there are far more important factors contributing to educational success than socio-economic status. Such factors include students' ability and motivation, a positive school environment, a challenging curriculum and effective pedagogy plus committed teachers who are subject experts.

The recent Productivity Commission report evaluating the current National School Reform Agreement concludes, despite the additional billions invested, educational outcomes have not significantly improved.

It's time to move on from fruitless debates about school funding and focus on the best way ensure all students, regardless of home background, achieve to the best of their ability. Making schools more competitive by adopting vouchers and giving schools autonomy is also the way ahead.

Give parents and students choice, not tired mantras

The Australian 28 January 2023

On the release of the Productivity Commission report detailing the failure of the latest National School Reform Agreement to lift standards and overcome disadvantage federal Education Minister Jason Clare argued "Serious reform is required... I don't want us to be a country where your chances in life depend on who your parents are, where you live, and the colour of your skin".

One of the truisms about education is if you teach long enough you will hear the same old clichés and empty promises from ministers year in and year out about raising standards and ensuring all students succeed regardless of where they live, ethnicity and home background.

There is nothing original about minister Clare's promise to raise standards and overcome disadvantage. Beginning with the Whitlam government's 1973 Karmel Report and the Disadvantaged Schools Programme Labor governments have repeatedly promised to raise standards and ensure all students, regardless of what school attended, achieve success.

In 2010 the education minister Julia Gillard when launching the My School website stated, "the Rudd government does not believe demography is destiny".

The justification for establishing the Gonski review of funding in 2010 that ended up spending $billions was to ensure students who lived in disadvantaged communities achieved success instead of students from wealthier, more privileged post codes always being on top.

In 2013, when Kevin Rudd was prime minister, the National Education Reform Agreement promised to ensure Australia's education system was "socially inclusive" and that it would reduce educational disadvantage suffered by indigenous and working class students.

The legislation associated with the reform agreement, once again, argued how well a student performs "should not be limited by where the student lives, the income of his or her family, the school he or she attends, or his or her personal circumstances".

Further evidence there is nothing new in minister Clare's promise any new agreement would set "targets for academic achievement" is the 2013 agreement that argued by 2025 Australia would be "in the top 5 highest performing countries: based on international reading, mathematics and science tests".

Linked to the 2013 reform agreement is the National Plan for School Improvement promising to improve teacher quality, ensure classroom practice was evidence based, all students succeeded and schools were publicly accountable for results.

The most recent national agreement set to run from 2019-2023 repeats the same mantra about ensuring Australian schools "provide a high quality and equitable education for all students".

The current reform agreement also promises to lift academic achievement for all students, especially disadvantaged, ensure all students are engaged in their learning and in a position to successfully "transition to further study and/or work and life success".

Once again, ignoring the evidence since the 2013 agreement Australian students have gone backwards in international tests, the current agreement promises Australia will have a "high quality and high equity schooling system by international standards by 2025".

Common to all the agreements over the last 20 years, and what minister Clare most likely plans for the next agreement, is the belief increased government intervention and bureaucratic oversight will lead to better results. As detailed by the recent Productivity Report such is not the case as educational outcomes have only gone backwards. Schools are drowning in red tape and intrusive and inflexible demands as a result of having to answer to two levels of government. Instead of having autonomy and flexibility, similar to charter schools in America and free schools in England, schools in Australia are forced to follow government dictates tied to funding.

There is a better alternative. Instead of politicians and bureaucrats far removed from the realities of the classroom imposing policy, schools and their communities based on the concept of subsidiarity are best placed to decide what must be done to meet students' needs.

School vouchers need to be introduced giving parents greater financial power to choose between schools, whether government or non-government. Increased parental choice leads to a more market driven system where schools are pressured to improve.

Instead of enforcing a Woke, new-age curriculum on schools, what is taught and what happens in the classroom must be academically rigorous, teacher friendly and based on what is effective.

Teacher training must be overhauled to ensure beginning teachers have the subject expertise and the skills and ability to deal with what is an ever increasing difficult and onerous classroom situation characterised by rowdy, disruptive students.

Underlying the cliché demography is not destiny and the argument all students deserve success is the mistaken belief all students have the same ability and motivation. The reality proves otherwise as some students, regardless of background, will always be more capable than others.

Loss of respect leaves education pointless

Daily Telegraph, 6 December 2022

Listen to teachers, parents and employers and a common complaint about the young is too many lack respect for authority as they believe they have the right to act and express themselves in any way they believe is acceptable.

Parents complain about rude children impossible to control, Australia has some of the most disruptive and badly behaved classrooms across the OECD and employers are forced to employ entitled young people who refuse to follow instructions.

In the streets and on public transport young people are often unnecessarily rude and boisterous and gone are the days of courteous behaviour where women and older people were treated with civility and respect.

The situation has deteriorated so markedly the Italian academic Augusto Del Noce in *The Crisis Of Modernity* writes "The eclipse of the idea of authority is one of the essential characteristics of today's world".

As evidence, Del Noce notes whereas the word authority originally referred to a process of growth towards a higher and more enriching understanding about human nature the word is now associated with repression and lack of freedom. Instead of authority being respected it is condemned.

Given such a change we now live in a world where individual entitlement and empowerment reigns supreme, where everyone is entitled to an opinion and where an uneducated, teenage girl is a climate change expert and able to lecture the United Nations and world leaders about how to save the planet.

The impact of social media outlets including Twitter (now X), Facebook and Instagram means anyone capable of getting on-line and using a keyboard is an instant expert capable of pontificating on any subject that takes his or her fancy. Regardless of how stupid or misplaced.

As noted by Del Noce, education and what happens in schools provides a striking example explaining why so many young people reject authority and feel they are entitled to do and say whatever they want, whenever they want.

Del Noce writes, instead of teachers being in control and the masters of their subject, "we have a kind of self-government of the young, who emancipate themselves from the burden of the past and use the teacher as an instructor in the methods of their liberation".

One if the defining features of Australian education is the adoption of a student-centred approach to learning, otherwise known as student agency, based on the belief students learn best when they are empowered to take control of their learning.

The move to undermine teacher authority can also be traced to the work of the Brazilian Marxist Paulo Freire who condemned traditional teachers as elitist and guilty of reinforcing capitalist hierarchy and privilege.

Instead of being authority figures teachers are now described as facilitators and guides by the side and in primary schools teachers no longer stand or sit at the front of the classroom. Students are knowledge navigators and digital natives who have the power to go on-line and self-educate.

Explicit teaching, where teachers direct learning on the basis they are in control and they are the experts, has given way to a process, inquiry-based approach where what students encounter is restricted to their immediate interests and what they see is relevant.

Beginning in primary school teacher unions and subject associations also tell teachers students must be empowered to become cultural-left warriors in controversial areas such as climate change, gender and sexuality and indigenous affairs.

Even the way students are assessed, where all are winners as failing students is counter-productive, contributes to young people's sense of entitlement and hostility towards authority. Teachers are told it's wrong to use letters A to E where E means fail and assessment must be negotiated, collaborative and descriptive. The Australian Education Union argues:

> *Reliance on competition is a primary cause of inequalities of educational outcome because students from certain social groups are advantaged by competitive selection methods. Competitive selection also sets students against each other rather than encouraging co-operative learning methods.*

Whereas education was once based on the belief students had to be initiated into an established body of knowledge, understanding and skills requiring humility, concentration, patience and hard work much of what now happens in the classroom involves edutainment.

Learning is immediately accessible, contemporary and relevant and as a result Del Noce argues "Schools no longer present themselves as institutions where teachers guide newcomers to an awareness of the civilisation that they must join and that they must continue".

Denying teacher authority and giving students unrestricted autonomy and freedom confuses the distinction between freedom from and freedom to. Giving students freedom from constraint means they lack the knowledge and skills necessary to achieve the freedom to be creative and to complete complex and difficult tasks.

Australia's dumbed down schools are going nowhere

Spectator Flat White, 21 October 2022

Over the last month there have been yet another two initiatives designed, supposedly, to improve the performance of Australian schools, raise standards and ensure greater equity. The first is an interim report by the Productivity Commission evaluating the 2018 National School Reform Agreement.

The NSRA is signed by commonwealth, state, and territory governments and details strategies designed to "lift student outcomes across Australian schools" by implementing a range of policies including a unique student identifier, reviewing senior secondary pathways and strengthening the initial teacher education accreditation system.

The second initiative involves establishing a panel to review the effectiveness of teacher training established by the Commonwealth Minister for Education Jason Clare and chaired by the ex-ABC Managing Director Mark Scott.

While applauded as the panacea to achieve excellence and equity both initiatives are destined to join a long list of reviews and reports beginning in the early 1970s that have proven counterproductive and worthless in strengthening Australia's education system.

Since the Karmel Report in 1973 and Victoria's Blackburn Report in 1985 there have been over 20 reviews and reports at all levels of government designed to strengthen schools, improve teacher effectiveness and raise standards.

Among the plethora commissioned are the Keating government's National Statements and Profiles (1992), the NSW's review of the Higher School Certificate (1995), a national inquiry into literacy teaching (2005), the Gonski Review of School funding (2011), the Review of the National Curriculum (2014), the Review to Achieve Educational Excellence (2017) and a review of the NSW curriculum (2020).

In addition to the eight state and territory education departments and curriculum bodies, in yet another attempt to improve Australia's substandard educational performance, the commonwealth government has also established the Australian Institute for Teaching and School Leadership (2005) and the Australian Curriculum and Assessment Authority (2008).

The dismal results of the last 50 years of reviews, reports, and government policies are obvious to all. Australia has slipped down the rankings as measured by the Programme for International Student Assessment (PISA) and the Trends in International Maths and Science Study (TIMSS) tests.

Apprentices start work with substandard literacy and numeracy skills, universities have dumbed-down first-year courses and too many students leave after 12 years of schooling culturally illiterate and morally adrift.

If those responsible for Australia's education system were in charge of a business they would have been sacked or gone broke. Instead, like the old industrial relations club, those responsible for the current malaise are reappointed to peak positions and given yet another chance to prove their ineptitude.

What's to be done? While the Greens Party, the Australian Education Union, and sympathetic academics argue what is needed in increased investment proven by the last 20 to 30 years spending more is simply throwing good money after bad.

It's also useless to establish yet another committee made up of bureaucrats and education department, teacher union, and subject association representatives who have minimal, if any, experience as practising teachers.

Until there are significant structural changes schools will continue to underperform, students will continue to suffer and the nation's cultural capital and productivity rates will continue to decline.

The first step is to realise there is no magic bullet and one-off reviews and reports focusing on a single issue like the curriculum, teacher training, how teachers are rewarded and classroom pedagogy will achieve nothing.

What determines school effectiveness and student achievement depends on a number of complex, interrelated factors that have to be addressed as a whole and at the same time.

Secondly, schools need to be freed from provider capture and what Michael Gove, when the British Secretary of State for Education, derided as the blob. Schools need greater autonomy and flexibility and less bureaucratic red tape and interference from on high.

The curriculum is overcrowded while the criteria-based, diagnostic assessment and reporting regime forces teachers to spend weeks writing voluminous descriptive reports. This is ineffective and takes energy away from teaching.

It should not surprise, proven by research by Australia's Gary Marks and overseas academics including Ludger Woessmann and Eric Hanushek, giving schools greater autonomy and flexibility allows non-government schools to outperform government schools.

The cutting edge of reform overseas involves charter schools in America, city academies and free schools in England plus charter schools in India. Such is their popularity in disadvantaged communities enrolments are oversubscribed.

For far too long Australia's education system has fallen victim to progressive, new-age fads including open classrooms, process and inquiry-based learning, student agency, teachers as facilitators and a curriculum driven by neo-Marxist inspired Woke ideology.

Schools have also been infected with the soft bigotry of low expectations where disadvantaged students are expected to always underperform. It's time to stop experimenting with unproven fads and ensure all schools embrace rigorous standards and high expectations.

Growing desire for a classical education

Daily Telegraph, 7 October 2022

Proven by a recent seminar in Melbourne where 30 parents, teachers, school leaders, academics and representatives from the Archdiocese of Melbourne and Catholic schools came together from around Australia to learn more about what constitutes a classical education, otherwise known as a liberal education, it's obvious what is happening overseas is also happening here.

Whether America, England or New Zealand, parents have decided the best way to ensure their children receive an enriching, substantial and rigorous education is to establish their own schools free of government control.

One of the reasons Ron DeSantis is Florida's governor and seen as a possible Republican presidential candidate is because he champions a balanced and impartial school curriculum; one increasing numbers of parents are organising to achieve.

The movement to oppose Woke ideology in schools and to reassert the value of an education based on what Matthew Arnold terms "the best that has been thought and said" also explains why Virginia now has a conservative Republican governor.

In England, such have been the fears state managed schools have lost their way Chris Woodhead, the former head of the government's school inspection body Ofsted, helped establish independent Cognita schools dedicated to character development and academic excellence.

Katherine Birbalsingh, the headteacher of the independent Michaela Community School, has also gained prominence for arguing there is no place for cultural-left ideology in education and schools must provide a disciplined environment based on high expectations.

Whether overseas or in Australia, parents are concerned about falling standards, lack of discipline, teachers being overworked and a curriculum that is superficial and characterised by progressive fads like child-centred, enquiry-based, 21st century learning.

Parents are also mobilising to establish their own schools as a result of the negative impact of critical theory and postmodernism where students are presented with a black armband view of society and Western civilisation.

In opposition to what is seen as a superficial and politically correct education those involved in the Melbourne seminar, organised by the Page Research Centre, argue the curriculum should embrace a classical, liberal view of education based on Western civilisation's best validated knowledge and artistic achievements.

The idea of a classical education can be traced to ancient Greece and Rome where what is central is the pursuit of truth, beauty and wisdom based on what the English philosopher Michael Oakeshott terms as a conversation in which students are encouraged to participate.

In order to participate productively students must first be familiar with texts such as *The Iliad, The Odyssey* and Greek tragedies including *Medea, Antigone* and *Oedipus*. Engaging in a Socratic dialogue where students are taught to evaluate and weigh arguments based on rationality and reason is also vital.

The various subjects and disciplines, whether music, art, mathematics, science, literature and history, while evolving over time, also embody essential knowledge, understanding and skills that must be taught in an explicit and substantial way.

Arguing students are knowledge navigators and digital natives and teachers are guides by the side and facilitators ignores the reality to be creative and critical thinkers students first need to be familiar with and master what is being taught.

As argued by the head of Sydney's liberal/arts Campion College Paul Morrissey, what also characterises a classical education is its focus on the four virtues so vital for the development of a student's character, what Aristotle describes as prudence, justice, temperance and courage.

At a time when students are surrounded by an ego-centred, narcissistic culture based on what is immediately gratifying and utilitarian teaching virtues grounds students in a more substantial, enriching and enduring set of beliefs and values.

A classical, liberal education, while drawing on the ancient world, also embodies a view of education based on the writings of Catholic theologians and philosophers including Thomas Aquinas and Saint Newman.

Both argue instead of education being restricted to what is contemporary, immediately relevant and utilitarian it should introduce students to a more enriching and engaging appreciation of the spiritual and transcendent.

For those parents committed to the Christian faith and the word of God such an education, by necessity, includes what the Bible says about how best to live the good life, what constitutes good and evil and the belief, with God's love and grace, all will be well.

At the Melbourne seminar parents, teachers and school leaders from Melbourne's Harkaway College, Sydney's Hartford College and the planned John Henry Newman College in Brisbane demonstrated what is happening overseas is also happening here.

Add the fact a number of teachers at the seminar have established the Australian Classical Education Society with links to the America's CIRCE Institute and it's clear the educational tide is slowly turning.

The barbarians are inside the gates

Quadrant Online, 5 October 2022 (This is an edited extract from Kevin's *The Dictionary Of Woke*)

How English is defined and taught as a subject illustrates how successful politically correct, Woke ideology has been in infecting the nation's schools. With learning how to read and write, drawing originally on the works of the South American Marxist Paulo Freire, the focus is very much on what is described a critical literacy.

Critical literacy argues learning a language and education more broadly must be emancipatory and liberating. The true purpose of education, in Freire's words, is to allow students "to perceive themselves in dialectical relationship with their social reality…to assume an increasingly critical attitude toward the world and so to transform it".

In 1974 Freire toured Australia and since that time academics in charge of teacher education and professional bodies like the Australian Association for the Teaching of English and the Australian Curriculum Studies Association have championed his radical philosophy.

An editorial written for a 2004 edition of *English in Australia* bemoaning the re-election of the conservative Howard Commonwealth Government illustrates how pervasive this Marxist inspired approach to English has become. The author, Wayne Sawyer, argues teachers had failed to adequately teach critical literacy and they must redouble their efforts as Howard being re-elected proved students were easily duped and not able to think clearly.

Sawyer argues, "What does it mean for us and our ability to create a questioning, critical generation that those who brought us balaclava'd security guards, Alsations and Patrick's Stevedoring could declare themselves the representatives of the workers and be supported by the electorate?".

Critical literacy and associated feminist, gender, sexuality and post-colonial theories have also had, and continue to have, a significant impact on how literature is now taught. Before the cultural-left's campaign to take control literature was generally restricted to those novels, short stories, plays and poems that had something significant, profound and lasting to say about human nature, how people interact and relate to the wider world and how we perceive and cope with the myriad challenges and issues we deal with as we journey through life.

Literature, especially Greek, Roman, Celtic and Norse myths, fables and legends, also deals with the predicaments, heroes, archetypes and feelings underpinning much of Western culture and that speak to our inner emotional and spiritual selves. What YB Yeats refers to as Spiritus Mundi. Such archetypes and myths deal with love, betrayal, courage, sorrow, forgiveness and the need to find a more spiritual and transcendent sense of meaning in what is an often unforgiving, transient and challenging world.

Instead of focusing on the moral and aesthetic importance of literature, one where students learn to understand human nature and to empathise with others, the emphasis is now on deconstructing texts in terms of power relationships and critical theory. In a paper delivered at a AATE National Conference, Maria Pallotta-Chiaarolli argues the English classroom must be re-positioned as "a site of deconstructionist and interventionist strategies when challenging/resisting dominant discourses of marginalistaion and prejudice". Examples of prejudice include "homophobia, heterosexism and AIDS-discrimination" along with "racism, ethnocentrism, classism and sexism".

How history is taught in schools has also been dramatically redefined to make it politically correct and Woke. While no one is suggesting schools and the curriculum should embrace an overly celebratory and positive approach, what the historian Geoffrey Blainey describes as a "three cheers view of history", what students are presented with undermines and critiques both Western civilisation and Australia's foundation as a penal colony and its evolution since 1788.

As detailed by Stuart Macintyre in *The History Wars* more radical approaches to teaching history emerged during the heady days of the Vietnam war moratoriums and the rise of the counter-culture movement. Macintyre writes:

In the 1960s and 1970s, critical approaches to Australian history questioned established interpretations of settlement and progress. Historians pursued voices frequently absent from the national narrative. Social historians of feminist, migrant and Aboriginal perspectives challenged the exclusiveness of traditional historical approaches.

How history is detailed in the Australian national curriculum from the preparatory to year 10 illustrates how successful the cultural-left has been in redefining the subject. Like other subjects, students are told in the history curriculum Australia is a multicultural, secular society characterised by diversity and difference and where various cultures, ethnic and race groups interact and live.

Even though Australia owes much to Western civilisation, Judeo-Christianity and Enlightenment values like rationality and reason the curriculum promotes a relativistic stance where all cultures and histories are treated equally and deserving of recognition and respect (except, of course, British and European). Even worse, it's possible for students to study history across years 7 to 10 without ever learning about ancient Egypt, Greece and Rome, medieval Europe and epochal events like the Renaissance and the Industrial Revolution.

Three of the cross-curricula priorities informing history, in addition to other subjects, are Aboriginal and Torres Strait Islander Histories and Cultures, Sustainability and Asia and Australia's Engagement with Asia. While there are literally hundreds of references to indigenous history, culture and spirituality the impact and significance of Western civilisation and Judeo-Christianity are treated in a superficial and fragmented fashion.

Christianity is rarely, if ever, mentioned and while the dark side of Western civilisation is emphasised (including slavery, mistreatment of women, the stolen generation, mandatory detention and the civil rights movement both in Australia and America), indigenous culture and history are presented in a positive light and beyond reproach.

In relation to Asia, and similar to the way indigenous culture and history is treated, students are presented with a sanitised picture. A picture that ignores and air brushes from history the millions starved, tortured and killed under dictators like Mao, Pol Pot and Ho Chi Minh. Whereas Australia is a Westminster, parliamentary democracy where people's rights and freedoms are protected there is also no mention in the national curriculum the majority of Asian countries are totalitarian, single party regimes where property can be confiscated and people imprisoned and denied the rights we take for granted without any protection or recourse.

Cultural relativism and identity politics prevail ignoring the reality Australia's political and legal institutions and much of our language, literature, music and art are inherited from Europe, Ireland and the United Kingdom. While the numbers are diminishing, it's also true Christianity is Australia's mainstream religion and the nation's political and legal institutions and way of life are indebted to Christianity.

The Road Ahead - In Darkness There is Light

Christianity cornerstone of Western civilisation

Daily Telegraph, 1 December 2023

For those shouting 'gas the Jews' and 'from the river to the sea, Palestine will be free', Ayaan Hirsi Ali's recent essay should be compulsory reading. Hirsi Ali, an internationally famous author and commentator who was raised as a Muslin and then became an atheist, explains why Christianity is central to the West's survival.

Hirsi Ali argues fundamentalist Islam, proven by Hamas' evil and barbaric actions in murdering and raping women and children, is inherently inhumane and destructive. Worse still, is the neo-Marxist inspired Woke epidemic that is undermining what makes Western civilisation so great.

Such is the existential threat facing Western countries represented by enemies within and without and the realisation our peace and security can no longer be guaranteed Hirsi Ali argues the West must especially acknowledge and defend Judeo-Christianity.

As a young girl living in Somalia, Hirsi Ali details how she and her friends were indoctrinated with a radical view of Islam preached by the terrorist group Islamic Brotherhood. Such groups preach a violent jihad against the West where non-believers are condemned as infidels and either killed, converted or heavily taxed.

Given the war in Gaza, it's significant Hirsi Ali writes "a special hatred was reserved for one subset of the unbeliever: the Jew". She says, "we cursed the Jew multiple times a day and expressed horror, disgust and anger at the litany of offences he had allegedly committed. The Jew had betrayed our Prophet".

Soon after the horrific 9/11 attack on New York's Twin Towers Ali Hirsi explains how the uncertainty and confusion arising from the terrorist attack led her to question the Islamic religion and, after discovering Bertrand Russell, why she became an atheist.

She writes "I found my cognitive dissonance easing. It was a relief to adopt an attitude of scepticism towards religious doctrine, discard my faith in God and declare no such entity existed. Best of all, I could reject the existence of hell and the danger of everlasting punishment".

After initially enjoying her new won freedom from religion Hirsi Ali realises such are the threats to Western nations like Australia what is needed is a belief system grounded in something more enduring, uplifting and morally and spiritually enriching.

She argues Russia's war in the Ukraine, China's threat to invade Taiwan, Islam's jihad or Holy War against unbelievers and the infectious spread of cultural-left ideology undermining Western civilisation cannot be opposed by military means or imposing sanctions and employing secular ideology.

Instead, she writes the only answer "lies in our desire to uphold the legacy of the Judeo-Christian religion. That legacy consists of an elaborate set of ideas and institutions to safeguard human life, freedom and dignity – from the nation state and the rule of law to the institutions of science, health and learning".

Judeo-Christianity provides a system of morality and truth underpinning concepts like the inherent dignity of the person, a commitment to social justice and the common good as well as individual freedom and freedom of conscience.

Such is the power of the Old and New Testaments one of the first actions carried out by totalitarian governments, whether communist or fascist, is to destroy the churches, kill the nuns and priests and burn the Bible.

The Italian Marxist Antonio Gramsci describes "socialism as the religion destined to kill Christianity" on the basis in order to be indoctrinated and controlled citizens must owe their allegiance to the Party and worship the earthly Supreme Ruler.

History tells us essential to any civilisation's prosperity, growth and survival is religion. To be human is to seek answers to such perennial questions as what's the meaning of life, why are we here on this earth, what happens after death and how do we find truth and justice.

What makes Western civilisation unique is Judeo-Christianity answers such questions. Hirsi Ali argues "I ultimately found life without any spiritual solace unendurable — indeed very nearly self-destructive. Atheism failed to answer a simple question: what is the meaning and purpose of life?"

What those thousands of students demonstrating in Sydney, Melbourne and Brisbane fail to realise is in defending Hamas and calling for Israel's destruction they are endorsing barbarism and evil while ignoring Israel's right to protect human life and defend liberty and freedom.

Islamic states like Iran, communist Russia and China as well as North Korea are oppressive, dictatorial regimes representing an axis of evil. In order to resist such darkness Hirsi Ali tells us we must find the light by acknowledging the West's patrimony and what makes us unique.

She writes "Unless we offer something as meaningful, I fear the erosion of our civilisation will continue. And fortunately, there is no need to look for some new-age concoction of medication and mindfulness. Christianity has it all".

Conservatism in a modern world?

Spectator Flat White, 29 August 2023

What does it mean to be a conservative? One interpretation characterises conservatism as ossified, backward-looking, and incapable of change. In politics, the Liberal Party is often condemned as old-fashioned and out of touch. To win elections all the Liberal Party has to do is to mimic the far-left agenda championed by the ALP, Greens and Teals in areas like climate change, gender and sexuality, identity politics, victimhood, and the Voice.

In education, instead of the essential knowledge, understanding, and skills inherited from the past, the body responsible for the national curriculum (ACARA) and like-minded academics argue the focus must be on content-free, 21st century competencies and skills as the future is unpredictable and ever-changing.

It's true conservatism values the past. Edmund Burke, who many consider the father of conservatism, describes British institutions and way of life as "an entailed inheritance derived from our forefathers".

Such is the need to acknowledge and celebrate the past, especially the British legal and political system, Burke concludes, "People will not look forward to prosperity who never look back to their ancestors".

At the same time Burke values the past it's also true he accepts the need for change. Burke argues "a state without the means of change is without the means of its conservation". Based on "the principle of improvement" Burke accepts societies cannot remain static.

The qualification though, and not unexpected given he was writing at the time of the French Revolution, is Burke prefers evolutionary change rather than revolutionary.

While dedicated to Liberty, Equality and Fraternity by violently overthrowing society's existing structures and institutions those responsible for the French Revolution sowed the seeds for a reign of violence and terror epitomised by Madame Guillotine and summary executions.

In opposition to violent change Burke cites the example of the British parliamentary and common law systems, since the time of *Magna Carta* and the Glorious Revolution, that limit the power of the monarchy and protect citizens' rights.

While acknowledging the need for evolutionary change, and similar to Edmund Burke, the Italian philosopher and cultural critic Augusto Del Noce argues against radical change involving a violent and sudden break with the past.

Del Noce describes such change as involving a "total revolution" and attributes its origins to Jean-Jacques Rousseau and Karl Marx.

In opposition to change directed at cancelling the past Del Noce endorses the principle "that the duration of a given country's institutions proves that they exist for a reason, and that modifications and improvements are possible within the context of such institutions".

Matthew Arnold also reinforces Burke's call for conservatism when, after referring to the need to be familiar with the "best that has been thought and said", he argues equally as vital is turning "a stream of fresh and free thought upon our stock notions and habits which we follow staunchly but mechanically".

Contrary to what critics argue the need to critique institutions and beliefs inherited from the past is an essential aspect of conservatism. The difference between conservatives and those committed to radical change is conservatives are sceptical of unwarranted change as it often causes more damage than good.

When detailing what characterises conservatism the English philosopher Michael Oakeshott differentiates between change and innovation. The type of change illustrated by a violent storm or the death of a friend, though regrettable, is to be accepted. What Oakeshott describes as innovation, on the other hand, involves human agency and design and, as such, has to be approached cautiously. Oakeshott writes:

> *Innovating is always an equivocal enterprise, in which gain and loss (even excluding the loss of familiarity) are so closely interwoven that it is exceedingly difficult to forecast the final up-shot: there is no such thing as unqualified improvement.*

As a consequence, Oakeshott lists a number of preconditions associated with innovation including those arguing for innovation must prove what they suggest is beneficial; what is proposed is gradual instead of being disruptive and violent; what is proposed addresses a specific shortcoming and any consequences, especially unintended ones, are evaluated for their impact.

The French Revolution and subsequent communist revolutions in Russia, China, Cuba, and Cambodia under Pol Pot prove the dangers of revolutionary change and the mistaken belief it is possible to cancel the past and establish a man-made utopia on this earth. Another example, while less violent and less brutal, illustrating the dangers of what Oakeshott describes as innovation is Australia turning its back on coal and gas in its race to renewable energy represented by solar and wind power.

Even though the race to reduce Australia's carbon footprint will have no impact on global emissions, involves billions of dollars of needless and wasteful expenditure and penalises those who can least afford soaring power bills, climate activists argue the nation must forge ahead.

A second example is the neo-Marxist belief gender and sexuality are social constructs and not biologically determined and God-given. Proven by the closure of Britain's gender clinic Tavistock and the over 1,000 families suing the clinic for malpractice it's clear transgender activism causes more harm than good.

The importance of a classical education

The Catholic Weekly, 5 July 2023

As Sydney's Campion College is one of the few tertiary institutions dedicated to the liberal/arts it should not surprise it was chosen as the location for a recent seminar dedicated to exploring the nature and importance of a classical school education.

Involving parents, teachers, academics and educationalists from across Australia, everywhere from Perth to Brisbane and Narre Warren to Toowoomba, discussion centred on the parlous state of the existing school curriculum and the need to provide a more intellectually challenging, morally grounded and spiritually uplifting education.

Speakers included Professor Tracey Rowland from Notre Dame University, Barry Spurr, former Professor of Poetry at the University of Sydney, Monica Doumit from the Sydney Archdiocese and columnist at the Catholic Weekly as well as the historian Dr Simon Kennedy and Rabbi Shimon Cohen who established the Institute for Judaism and Civilisation.

Also attending the seminar were those either involved in already existing schools or facing the challenge of establishing their own schools dedicated to a classical education. Examples include Hartford College in Sydney, St John Henry College in Brisbane and Harkaway Hills College in Melbourne.

The first presentation argued existing models of school education ranging from a student centred approach to one focused on teaching generic skills and 21st century competencies failed to address the more urgent need to initiate each succeeding generation into the culture in which they are born.

As argued by the American academic Christopher J Lucas, "education basically means enculturation. The culture of a society must be internalised by each generation". Such an education does not happen intuitively or by accident and, while parents are their children's primary educators, schools have a significant role to play.

On the basis the purpose of education is enculturation the challenge then is to decide what type of education is the most relevant and the best able to provide students with a rigorous and beneficial school experience.

Professor Tracey Rowland, in addressing such a challenge, explores the concept of a classical education that has a number of defining characteristics. Instead of being utilitarian and practical such as education is associated with "the acquisition of a table of virtues, habits and dispositions".

Seen through a Christian perspective Rowland also suggests a classical education seeks to enrich and cultivate "the intellect, the will, the memory, the imagination and the affective dimension of the soul".

Much like Saint John Henry Newman's concept of a liberal education the ideal of a classical education is to educate students "who have a sense of place in history, who are not prisoners of their own time and culture, but have an understanding of the philosophical and theological traditions of Western culture and its history" so they can better deal with contemporary issues.

As argued by the third speaker, Rabbi Shimon Cohen, the challenge for parents and teachers seeking a classical education is students live in a society where there "is no cognizance of the spiritual as a factor or dimension of the human being".

Even worse, while the road map for Australian schools the Alice Springs Declaration mentions the importance of spirituality, contemporary education is based on the premise "the child has no soul" and there is no place for religion in the curriculum.

In opposition to the radical secularism that prevails in the curriculum, best illustrated by the neo-Marxist inspired Safe Schools gender fluidity program, Cohen argues it is time to reassert the central importance of the spiritual and the transcendent only a commitment to a higher good can provide.

Cowen, drawing on the work of Viktor Frankel, describes this as "the awakening of the highest faculty in the human being, the soul or conscience through the practice of self-transcendence". Rather than associating this transcendence with one religion, Cowen suggests it draws on the Noahide laws.

Such laws provide the basis for a universal ethics teaching "the true, the beautiful and the good" that underpins the world's great religions as well the concept of a classical education that first appeared in ancient Greece and Rome. As a result, it is relevant to people of religious faith as well as those more secularly minded.

While the morning session of the seminar explored the purpose of education and what constitutes a classical, liberal/arts curriculum, the afternoon session dealt with more practical matters. Topics included the legal challenges faced by faith-based schools, presentations from those involved in establishing schools and classroom teachers detailing their experiences.

As noted by Monica Doumit, given the extreme secular nature of society where many argue religious schools cannot exercise control over enrolments, staffing and what is taught, those in charge of such schools need to be wary of possible pitfalls.

In relation to enrolment forms and employment contracts, and proven by the example of Brisbane's Citipointe Christian where the principal was pressured to resign, schools need to ensure they have clear and well-argued legal advice on what is acceptable and what is not according to the law.

Faith-based schools also need to be aware of how best to manage and deal with adverse publicity in case they become embroiled in controversy as a result of public campaigns to undermine their autonomy and the inherent right they have to religious freedom.

There's no doubt the world young people are growing up in is fraught with difficulties and challenges. Evidenced by growing rates of anxiety, depression and disengagement, it is also true young people lack a sense of resilience and optimism about the future.

What a classical, liberal/arts education provides is the ability to cope with adversity, a strong sense of what constitutes right and wrong and a commitment to the common good. As argued by Roger Scruton, such an education also passes on to future generations, "an intellectual and artistic patrimony". A patrimony that involves the "accumulation of art, literature and humane reflection that has stood the test of time and established a continuing tradition of reference and allusion among educated people".

Events like the recent classical education and schools seminar illustrate how, around Australia, parents, teachers and school leaders are starting small fires and ensuring there is hope and optimism for the future.

Looking backwards leads us forwards

Catholic Weekly, 13 March 2023

One of the tropes used by the cultural-left when denigrating conservatism is to attack it as backward looking, ossified and irrelevant.   At the same time neo-Marxist inspired activists argue the history of Western civilisation is riven with injustice, oppression and violence against what Edward Said describes as the 'other'.

The global move to cancel the past by decolonising the curriculum is based on the belief the history of Western civilisation is awash with imperialism and racism leading to the subjugation and oppression of indigenous people in what is now Africa, Australia, South America and Indo-China.

The reality, instead of being backward looking, is conservatism acknowledges the need for change.   Edmund Burke, often described as the father of conservatism, writes being a member of society involves a partnership "between those who are living, those who are dead, and those who are to be born".

Burke's warning "People will not look forward to posterity, who never look backward to their ancestors" is especially true in relation to the French Revolution beginning in 1789 that pulled down the Ancient Regime and the Catholic Church and replaced both with Madame Guillotine and the reign of terror.

Conservatism is not reactionary searching for a lost golden age but, instead, is based on the conviction Western civilisation, as does Aboriginal and Torres Strait culture, has its roots in the past.   It's institutions and way of life did not magically appear but have evolved over countless generations.

The origins of our political and legal system provides an illustration. Notwithstanding government totalitarian overreach as a result of Covid-19 Australia compared to Russia, China and Iran, is relatively peaceful and stable where rights are protected, all are able to vote and the rule of law prevails.

Such an approach to governance has evolved over time and has its antecedents in the past drawing on British common law, a Westminster parliamentary system and documents like the 1215 *Magna Carta* and the 1689 Bill of Rights.

As detailed in David Kemp's *The Land Of Dreams* when the First Fleet arrived in 1788 the fledging colony was lucky enough to inherit a system of government and legal rights considered "one of the wonders of Europe".

This was a time when the rule of law became preeminent and the right to liberty and freedom became widespread. That a married convict couple who arrived with the First Fleet won a court case against the captain of their ship for losing their possessions illustrates the value of what we have inherited.

As noted by Larry Siedentop in *Inventing the Individual: the Origins of Western Liberalism*, the form of government the penal settlement inherited also drew on Christ's teaching as all individuals are made in God's image all deserve freedom, justice and the right to live their lives free of oppression and tyranny.

With expressions like love thy neighbour as thyself and "There is neither Jew nor Greek, there is neither bond nor free, there is neither male nor female: for ye are all one in Christ Jesus" it should not surprise Arthur Phillip argued there would be no slavery in the new colony and Aborigines should be treated fairly.

Instead of acknowledging, for all its sins and faults, Western nations like Australia over time have evolved into beacons of prosperity and peace in an increasingly hostile world cultural-left activists, especially those committed to post-colonial theory, denigrate and vilify our institutions and way of life.

At the tertiary level proven by a survey by the Institute of Public Affairs evaluating 791 courses across 35 Australian universities, not surprisingly, what students encounter is dominated by neo-Marxist inspired critical race theory and identity politics.

Whereas school history once traced the evolution of civilisation from Mesopotamia and Egypt to the Greeks and Romans and then to what is now Europe and the United

Kingdom students are now presented with a smorgasbord of Woke topics seen through indigenous, environmental and Asian perspectives. Christianity is rarely, if ever, mentioned.

While indigenous activists promoting the Voice to parliament argue Aboriginal and Torres Strait Islander history and elders must be acknowledged and celebrated they fail to show the same respect and appreciation for Australia's British heritage and the debt owed to the European civilisation.

Activists also ignore the reality there is much about indigenous history and culture that is violent, patriarchal and oppressive.

A light to all the world

Quadrant Online, 25 December 2022

Evidenced by the colourful decorations in shopping centres and images of Father Christmas and his reindeers, the late minute rush to buy presents for family and friends and the arrival of the summer school holidays, it's obvious Christmas is upon us. As such, it's a good time to ask what is the meaning of Christmas and why do so many Western countries like Australia celebrate the 25th of December as such a memorable day? In the same way Aboriginal activists argue for truth-telling about indigenous history, culture and their celebrations the same can be said for this nation's Western heritage.

To survive and prosper societies need a strong moral and spiritual belief system that fashions human behaviour and how we interact with others. In the same way we acknowledge indigenous peoples and their unique culture and spirituality it's only right we do the same for Australia's mainstream culture.

Christmas is seen by many as a time to give and receive gifts, to share hospitality with family and friends and to start that much needed holiday free from worry and stress. For Christians, though, the birth of Jesus represents an epochal event radically transforming history and the way we live.

As suggested by Pope Francis, "Standing before the manger, we understand that the food of life is not material riches but love. Not gluttony but charity, not ostentation but simplicity". The Christian message is to love thy neighbour as thyself and, as the Good Samaritan demonstrated, to show charity and sympathy to others.

When explaining the significance of Christmas Pope John Paul 11 stated, "Jesus is born for a humanity searching for freedom and peace. He is born for everyone burdened by sin, in need of salvation, and yearning for hope". In a dangerous world where evil and temptation exist Jesus' teachings offer a guiding light illuminating the darkness.

While many argue Australia is a secular society and insist we now live in a post-Christian age the reality is our heritage is a Christian one that underpins and enriches our institutions and way of life. While it's true since Federation in 1901 the percentage of Australians identifying as believers has declined, Christianity at 43.9 per cent of the population is still the most popular religion.

Parliaments around Australia begin with the Lord's Prayer and it's no accident the preamble to the Australian Constitution includes the phrase "Humbly relying on the blessing of Almighty God". Our legal institutions are also underpinned by Christian teachings beginning with the Ten Commandments. While people now have a choice, for countless years anyone giving evidence in court swore on the Bible and Christian concepts such as redemption and forgiveness explain why convicted criminals, often through good behaviour and repentance, are offered reprieves on their sentences.

Especially at this time of year and in our current economic climate, where so many are suffering disadvantage and poverty, it is Christian managed or inspired organisations like the Salvation Army, Caritas, the St Vincent de Paul Society and Mission Australia providing so much comfort and support.

The poet T S Eliot in his essay *Notes Towards a Definition of Culture* argues even those who are not religious have to recognise Christianity's impact on the arts, especially literature, music, architecture, sculpture and painting plus "our conceptions of private and public morality". Eliot also argues religion, whether Hinduism, Judaism, Buddhism or Islam, is an essential aspect of any worthwhile and healthy culture and, in relation to Western nations like Australia, he warned "If Christianity goes, the whole of our culture goes".

While it's difficult to prove the two things are connected, it should not surprise at the same time the number of Australians identifying as Christian has declined society has seen a significant increase in rates of anxiety, depression and self-harm, the incidence of alcohol and drug abuse and the rise of single-parent families. Add domestic violence and the destructive impact of pornography and sexualisation of childhood and there is a no doubt too many people lack the moral compass and spiritual awareness that Christianity provides.

Jesus teaches while this world is far from perfect and people are prone to suffering, pain and sin, not all is lost. With the power of prayer there is redemption and forgiveness and the joy that comes from embracing God's love.

Christmas is a time for celebrating with family and friends and giving and receiving gifts, at the same time it is vital to remember the greatest gift is the birth of Jesus and the promise of eternal salvation in the world to come.

In times of darkness there is always light

Daily Telegraph, 14 October 2022

Last week, October 10th was world mental health day and if there was ever a time for Australians to focus on the issue this is it. Especially after the last 3 years of China-virus induced dislocation, loss of freedom, school closures, bankruptcies and government over-reach ever increasing numbers of Australians are at risk.

According to the 2021 national census the most common health issue is mental illness with 2,231,543 Australians affected. A more recent ABS survey also paints a disturbing picture with

43.7 per cent of Australians aged 16-85 experiencing a mental disorder.

Titled the *National Study of Mental Health and Wellbeing* the study concludes the most common forms of mental disorder include anxiety, depression and substance abuse. The suicide rate is especially alarming with 8 Australians, on average, ending their lives each day.

While mental health disorders affect all age groups young people are especially vulnerable. At a time when they should be optimistic and positive 39.6 per cent of young adults suffer panic attacks, social phobia, post-traumatic stress and being obsessive-compulsive.

While much of the left-leaning media and politicians argue females are victims of a hostile, male dominated society, it's also alarming males, compared to females, are more likely to suffer physical violence and have higher rates of substance abuse and suicide.

While more women experience intimate partner violence, 19.2 compared to 7 percent suffered by men, if you include violence from other people and strangers the situation is reversed with 40.8 per cent of men aged 18 years an older at risk compared to 30.5 per cent of females.

Men, especially young men and teenagers, also have higher rates of suicide compared to females. According to Lifeline 75 per cent of those committing suicide are men, far exceeding the numbers caused by road accidents.

Such is the prevalence of anxiety and depression it should not surprise Australia has such high rates of alcohol and drug abuse. According to the Criminal Intelligence Commission Australia has the highest methylamphetamine (ice) consumption per head of population compared to 24 other countries.

Research suggests 33 per cent of Australians regularly exceed the recommended daily use of alcohol leading to the situation where the impact of alcohol abuse amounts to $64 billion a year in terms of health, workplace, road accident and personal costs.

Add other drugs including opioids, cannabis, ecstasy and cocaine and there is no doubt Australia is suffering a drug and alcohol induced epidemic even more destructive than the China-virus.

What's to be done? Viktor Frankel, who was imprisoned in Nazi concentration camps during the second world war and who suffered and witnessed unspeakable acts of cruelty, suggests those who survived held on to a more spiritual and transcendent view of life.

While acknowledging suffering and pain are ever present Frankel writes those who had religious faith understood "the hopelessness of our struggle did not detract from its dignity and its meaning".

It's vital to recognise no matter how isolated and despondent one feels one is never alone. Comfort and reassurance comes from the love of family and friends and the belief not all is lost.

Bruno Bettelheim was another who experienced the horror of concentration camps and he argues to be resilient and able to deal with adversity children from an early age must encounter the myths, fables and stories dealing with loss and suffering and that teach optimism and courage.

Aesop's fables, stories from the Brothers Grimm and enduring literary texts like *The Iliad* and *The Odyssey* and more recent ones including the *Narnia* series by CS Lewis and Tolkien's *Lord of the Rings* have much to teach.

Instead of being surrounded by digital technology where hours are wasted on social networking sites and in front of screens children also need to be physically active, to take risks and to play competitive sports where they learn how to cope with defeat.

Schools, instead of being consumed with identity politics and victimhood, need to teach students life inevitably involves set-backs and losses and the challenge is how one copes with what Shakespeare describes as "the slings and arrows of outrageous fortune".

After losing our son James in a hit and run accident I've experienced first-hand how cruel, unforgiving and senseless life can be. At the same time, while there is never closure, it is possible to endure and to find solace.

Acknowledging one's responsibility to others, finding comfort in the love of family and understanding how fulfilling and enjoyable life can still be tempers the loss. Religious faith is also important. As argued by Julian of Norwich, with God's love and grace, "All shall be well, and all shall be well, and all manner of thing shall be well".

Woke world is wobbling

Daily Telegraph, 2 September 2022

It's clear those championing today's Wear It Purple day and arguing schools and universities embrace LGBTIQ+ gender ideology have no idea of the overseas push back when it comes to telling children and teenagers it's OK to change their birth sex and undergo gender transitioning.

In championing radical gender theory based on the belief Australian society is guilty of being heteronormative and transphobic the Australian Education Union, the Australian Association for the Teaching of English, the ABC and the Sydney Morning Herald also ignore recent overseas events.

In Britain, the gender fluidity clinic Tavistock was recently closed after an inquiry concluded allowing often confused and immature children to transition to another gender was unacceptable.

Reports suggest up to 1000 parents plan to sue Tavistock and the medical practitioners involved for negligence for failing to counsel children and teenagers about the harmful consequences of taking puberty blockers.

While in Australia the Kid's Help Line and the commonwealth's discussion paper for kindergartens push LGBTIQ+ ideology, the British cabinet minister Suella Braverman argues schools must stop pushing radical gender theory on vulnerable children.

Braverman argues "Schools have a duty of care in relation to the health, safety, and welfare of their children and they risk breaching this duty when they encourage and facilitate a child's social transition as a blanket policy; or take the decision to do so without medical advice".

In Sweden and Finland, often championed as socially progressive, health professionals, instead of automatically endorsing transitioning, have been told young people must be made aware of the dangers of taking puberty blockers and undergoing life changing surgery.

As a result of parental and community pressure in Florida, Virginia and a number of other American states governments are legislating to stop kindergartens and schools from imposing gender ideology on children too young to understand such abstract concepts.

Based on overseas events it's obvious sanity and common sense are beginning to prevail on the basis sex is biologically determined and not a matter of self-identification. In Australia, neo-Marxist inspired LGBTIQ+ activists still dominate.

Christian schools are publicly attacked and threatened with having their funding cut for simply asserting what, according to their religious beliefs, is incontrovertible as according to the Bible God created man and woman.

In NSW school principals are told "If either or both parents object to the change to the way the first name is recorded by the school, the principal needs to make a decision about what is in the child's best interests".

Principals are also told transgender students should be allowed to use the toilets and changing rooms of the sex they self-identify as and if students complain about having to share facilities with transgender students they should be re-educated by the "school learning and support team".

The University of Sydney is only one of the many universities supporting radical gender ideology and events like Wear It Purple Day. The university has established a Pride

Network to "challenge homophobia, transphobia and biphobia and homophobic attitudes and behaviours".

Victoria's education department is 100 per cent behind events like Wear It Purple Day by announcing "This year, for the first time, the Victorian Public Sector (VPS) LGBTIQ+ Pride Awards will be celebrated on Wear it Purple Day" and awarding prizes for Woke teachers and departmental bureaucrats.

The organisation responsible for Victoria's school curriculum, the VCAA, also celebrates and acknowledges Wear It Purple day on the basis LGBTIQ+ students suffer "discrimination and prejudice" proven by the fact such students are the victims of "verbal homophobic abuse".

Over the last 10 years the Safe Schools program has told students Australian society is guilty of homophobia, transphobia and heteronormativity and the way to achieve sexual freedom is to embrace what Roz Ward describes as a world where "bodies can blossom in extraordinary, new and amazing ways that we can only try to imagine today".

Even worse, notwithstanding events surrounding Tavistock, in Victoria Chairman Dan has legislated to stop parents, priests and health professionals from counselling young people about the dangers and harmful consequences of taking puberty blockers.

Thankfully, the days when gays and lesbians were victimised and society punished any who did not conform to often inflexible sexual stereotypes have long since gone. The majority of Australians embraced same-sex marriage and the law protects all regardless of gender and sexuality.

The danger, instead of accepting such changes and the reality gender and sexuality are biologically determined, is gender activists seek to indoctrinate young people with an ideology that is often harmful and counter-productive.

As a result, children are denied the innocence of youth and parents denied the right they have as a child's guardians to decide what is best when it comes to such controversial issues.

Let's fight for rational thought and common sense

Daily Telegraph, 8 September 2022

Woke activists championing politically correct language and group think justify their actions by arguing it's the best way to overcome disadvantage and rid society of prejudice and unfair discrimination.

Nothing could be further from the truth. Recent events prove any who criticise or question cultural-left group think are immediately condemned and cancelled.

As a result of the cultural-left's long march language has been weaponised as an instrument to silence debate and to condition people to accept what the thought police determine is true, no matter how contradictory, illogical or unreasonable.

Question multiculturalism and rates of immigration and you are condemned as racist and xenophobic, suggest it's OK for women to be feminine and you are sexist and any who defend Western civilisation are guilty of European supremacy and whiteness.

Argue gender and sexuality are inherently biological and it's wrong to automatically assume it's OK for teenagers to take puberty blockers and undergo life changing surgery and you are transphobic and guilty of heterosexism.

While pretending to preach tolerance and respect for diverse opinions, the reality is cultural-left activists are always intolerant and only concerned with silencing and cancelling any who disagree or fail to conform.

As well as stifling freedom of expression and the ability to debate in a reasonable and balanced way political correctness and Woke ideology are also guilty of attacking and undermining what is best about Western civilisation and the institutions on which our freedoms depend.

In schools and universities students are taught there is nothing redeeming or beneficial about the nation's history. What Geoffrey Blainey describes as a black armband view dominates where Captain Cook is an imperialist, the First Fleet an invasion and our legal and economic systems riven with structural racism, sexism and transphobia.

Boys in primary and secondary schools are taught men are misogynist and violent and they need to apologise for being male. Girls are taught there is nothing preferable about being a wife and a mother and the only way to prove their worth is to focus on their careers.

Christianity is vilified and condemned and banished from the public square. Ignored is the New Testament teaching the importance of virtues like wisdom, courage, moderation and love and the belief every person deserves justice and liberty.

Faith-based schools upholding their religious convictions and scientists arguing sexuality is biologically determined are especially targeted and publicly attacked and accused of hate speech.

Such is the dominance of left-of-centre group think, where rationality and reason no longer apply, even science has fallen victim to the thought police. In the UK universities have embarked on a campaign to decolonise what is attacked as a Eurocentric, white science curriculum.

Academics at the University of Sheffield argue Western science is guilty of being "inherently white" and complicit in "European Imperialism and a major beneficiary of its injustices". Enlightenment science is also seen as complicit in "racism and the injustices of colonisation".

The UK science journal 'Nature Human Behaviour' argues to be ethical any research, in addition to respecting the rights of people, should "respect the rights of non-human life, tangible and intangible heritage, natural resources and the environment".

In addition to the difficulties in identifying how a rock or a tree might be harmed by unethical research the question has to be asked, isn't the primary role of science to be impartial and objective and to seek what constitutes the truth, regardless of what PC dictates.

The school curriculum is not immune as proven by recent events in New Zealand. In a paper suggesting changes to science teaching the statement is made "science has been used to support the dominance of Eurocentric views (including) its use as a rationale for the colonisation of Māori".

In order to decolonise the curriculum, the argument is Māori science is equally as important and beneficial as Western science and any who disagree must be silenced as they have never experienced the "intergenerational dispossession and denigration" suffered by New Zealand's indigenous people.

As well as corrupting the English language cultural-left ideology champions identity politics where so-called disadvantaged individuals and groups, such as women, LGBTIQ+ and indigenous people and those of colour, are presented as victims made powerless by an oppressive system.

Ignored, compared to totalitarian dictatorships including Russia, China, North Korea and Iran is Western nations like Australia are open and free societies where rights and liberties are protected.

It's time to fight back and to reassert the strengths and benefits of Western civilisation and Western, liberal democracies like Australia. It's also time to reassert the importance of rationality, reason and common sense instead on neo-Marxist inspired indoctrination and group think.

Fashionable no, but religion's not dead yet

Herald Sun, 6 July 2022

On reading about his death Mark Twain replied, "the report of my death was an exaggeration". For those commentators arguing Christianity and the Catholic Church are mortally wounded based on the 2021 census results regarding religion the same response applies.

With newspaper headlines like "Abandoning God: Christianity plummets as 'non-religious' surges in census", "Losing our religion as Christianity plummets" and comments like "Australia has become strikingly more godless over the last decade", it would be easy to conclude religion is in its death throes.

Nothing could be further from the truth. While there's no doubt the number of Australians identifying as Christian has declined from 52% in 2016 to just under 44% in the 2021 census religion is still a powerful and potent force in Australia.

With older Australians some 60% have a religious affiliation and during the 2 years of the Covid-19 crisis, when churches were not forced to close, there was a noticeable improvement in attendance. It's also true religious schools, hospitals, aged care facilities, charities and social welfare organisations underpin and enrich Australian society.

Contrary to what Heidi Nicholl, the CEO of Humanists Australia, argues in a column published in *The Sydney Morning Herald* that religious organisations should no longer be tax exempt, the reality is without such mainly Christian bodies Australia's social, health and educational fabric would unravel.

As noted by Australia's one-time deputy prime minister John Anderson it's also true Australia's political and legal systems, plus much of our music, literature and art is deeply imbued with Christian beliefs and virtues, especially the New Testament. Concepts like liberty and freedom and committing to social justice and the common good are Christian in origin.

Instead of heralding the demise of Christianity what secular critics should contemplate is what the latest census tells us about what is described as an increasingly godless society. The census reveals mental health tops the list ahead of asthma and arthritis as the most common health problem.

While exacerbated by the Covid-19 pandemic there is no doubt Australians, especially young men where suicide is the most common form of death, are suffering high levels of anxiety and depression.

It's also true Australia is suffering a drug epidemic where, in addition to hard drugs including cannabis, cocaine and ecstasy, high rates of opioid addiction and alcoholism indicate widespread anxiety and societal breakdown.

While religion is not guaranteed as a panacea enabling one to cope with the traumas, self-doubt, suffering and pain life inevitably brings, believing in the spiritual and transcendent and that Jesus suffered on the cross for our sakes provides reassurance and comfort not all is lost.

As argued by the Christian mystic Teresa of Avila, "Let nothing disturb you. Let nothing frighten you. Everything passes away except God". Julian of Norwich argues in a similar fashion when she writes, "all shall be well, and all shall be well and all manner of thing shall be well".

The author of *The Gulag Archipelago*, Aleksandr Solzhenitsyn, when explaining the millions killed and starved under communism and fascism argues the reason is "Men have forgotten God. The failings of human consciousness, deprived of its divine dimension, have been a determining factor in all the major crimes of this century".

Long seen as a vitally important social institution marriage is also in poor health with the census revealing there are now one million single parent families where 75% of the single parents are women. As a product of a broken family where our mother was forced to cope after dad left, I know from personal experience growing up with two parents is preferable.

Children raised by both parents, in the majority of cases, offers a stable and secure upbringing. The research shows boys, in particular, need strong, positive fathers who mentor their sons about what constitutes virtuous masculinity and how best to lead a fulfilling and enriching life.

There's no doubt since the birth of Christ those professing to be Christians have been guilty of a multitude of sins. Whether the Spanish Inquisition, the pogroms against the Jews or the corruption of medieval and Renaissance popes, there is much to forgive. Include the evil crime of paedophilia and there's no doubt secular critics are right to criticise Christianity and the Church.

At the same time it is important to appreciate the inherent value of Christian morals and virtues and the way Christianity underpins our institutions and way of life. Equally as important, in an increasingly materialistic and sterile world, is the need to experience the spiritual and transcendent.

As the Bible states, "man does not live by bread alone" and whether Michelangelo's *Pietà*, Rachmaninov's *Vespers*, Milton's *Paradise Lost* or Dostoyevsky's *Crime and Punishment*, Christianity offers a window to human flourishing and a sense of the divine.

Great minds agree: preserve the tried, tested and true

The Australian, 18 June 2022

What is conservatism and what does it mean to be conservative? Given the defeat of the Liberal/National government and the arguments put by LINOs including Simon Birmingham the Liberal Party must be more progressive and less centre-right the issue is more than academic.

In his essay 'On Being a Conservative' Michael Oakeshott writes to be conservative, instead of involving a "creed or doctrine", involves a particular disposition. A disposition characterised by "certain kinds of conduct and certain conditions of human circumstance to others".

A disposition, instead of chasing utopian dreams, content with what exists no matter how imperfect and that acknowledges the inheritance passed from one generation to the next. Oakeshott suggests being conservative "is to prefer the familiar to the unknown, to prefer the tried to the untried, fact to mystery, the actual to the possible, the limited to the unbounded...".

The incessant call for change ignores the reality not all change is beneficial as there are often unforeseen and unintended consequences. The rush to adopt 21st century digital technologies including social networking sites ignores the negative impact on how people interact and socialise. A virtual world can never replace face to face contact.

One of the tropes used to criticise conservatism is the argument it is ossified and backward looking. While it's true conservatives value the past and the importance of tradition it is equally true conservatism is forward looking and capable of evolving over time.

Matthew Arnold in *Culture and Anarchy*, when detailing what constitutes a worthwhile culture, uses the phrase "the best which has been thought and said in the world". As important as established knowledge and understanding is what Arnold describes as turning "a stream of fresh and free thought upon our stock notions and habits, which we now follow staunchly, but mechanically…".

The need to continually test and evaluate what is passed from one generation to the next is also argued by the Italian philosopher and cultural critic Augusto Del Noce. When distinguishing between reactionaries and conservatives Del Noce observes while the former yearns to return to a lost golden age the second accepts the present will always be different to the past.

Unlike revolutionary ideologies underpinning epochal events like the French and Russian revolutions Del Noce also argues conservatism represents a:

> … *critique of utopia, of the idea that it is possible to achieve a worldly situation in which all contradictions have been solved, and to create conditions in which there is perfect harmony between virtue and happiness.*

Whereas utopian, materialistic ideologies lead to oppression and domination Del Noce defines conservatism "in the best sense as conservation of freedom". The British cultural critic Roger Scruton also associates conservatism with freedom. Scruton argues:

> *For the conservative, human beings come into this world burdened by obligations, and subject to institutions and traditions that contain within them a precious inheritance of wisdom, without which the exercise of freedom is likely to destroy human rights and entitlements as to enhance them.*

Drawing on Edmund Burke, Scruton also writes:

> *Society, he argued, does not contain the living only; it is an association between the dead, the living and the unborn... It is a shared inheritance for the sake of which we learn to circumscribe our demands, to see our place in things as part of a continuous chain of giving and receiving.*

The irony is while the Woke, cultural-left champions Aboriginal heritage and traditions in what is taught in schools and universities, the very Western civilisation underpinning and nourishing Australian society is denigrated and attacked as Eurocentric, obsolete and of no benefit or value.

After detailing the destructive impact of politically correct ideology Scruton argues underlying conservatism is the "conviction good things are more easily destroyed than created, and the determination to hold on to things in the face of politically engineered change".

While Scruton is writing about culture the current energy crisis facing the nation, where the rush to so-called clean, renewable energy and the campaign to vilify coal and gas as much needed reliable sources of power, illustrates the dangers of embracing policies based on progressive politically engineered change.

While much of the post second world war intellectual debate has focused on the battle between communism and capitalism Scruton also makes the point the current battle of ideas is between political correctness, since redefined as being Woke, and what he terms "cultural conservatism".

Scruton writes conservatives have, "turned in a new direction, exploring the roots of secular government in the Christian inheritance, and the place of religion in society which has made freedom of conscience into one of its ruling principles".

After referring to Samuel P. Huntington's *The Clash of Civilisations and the Making of World Order* Scruton argues Western societies have to regain "confidence not in our political institutions only, but in the spiritual inheritance on which they ultimately rest". A lesson the Liberal Party needs to learn.

The spirit of conservative vision

Spectator Flat White, 14 May 2022

One of the principal election strategies employed by Scott Morrison is the argument that Anthony Albanese and the Labor Party cannot be trusted with the economy as Liberal governments are better economic and financial managers.

Since the time of Robert Menzies capitalism and the free market have been viewed as preferable to socialism and centralised state control.

Ignored, as the Bible says, "Man shall not live by bread alone". To be human is to thirst for a more lasting, more profound, and more visionary sense of the world and one's place in it. The need to reassert the importance of a more substantial sense of how to find fulfilment and meaning is especially needed given the impact of neo-Marxist inspired political correctness and cancel culture.

As argued by the British philosopher and cultural critic Roger Scruton, such is the impact of the culture wars it is no longer enough for political leaders to focus on issues like market economics and free trade.

In his book *Conservatism* Scruton writes the challenge facing conservatives is to reassert the significance of Christianity. Scruton exhorts conservatives to:

> *Rediscover what we are and what we stand for, and having rediscovered it, be prepared to fight for it. That is now, as it has ever been, the conservative message. And what we stand for is a religious as much as political inheritance.*

Scruton goes on to suggest central to the conflict between conservatism and cultural Marxism is the process of "exploring the roots of secular government in the Christian inheritance" and re-establishing "confidence, not in our political institutions only, but in the spiritual inheritance on which they ultimately rest".

As argued by Augusto Zimmermann in his chapter *Why Christianity Matters In These Troubled Times,* it is impossible to appreciate and understand the political and legal systems Australia has inherited from Britain without acknowledging Christ's teachings in the New Testament.

Christian concepts like the inherent dignity of the person, the right to liberty and freedom, and the belief God's laws are above the laws of the State, underpin documents like *Magna Carta* and the American *Declaration of Independence*. It's no accident Christians like William Wilberforce led the campaign to end slavery and Martin Luther King's *I Have a Dream* speech is imbued with Christian teachings.

As noted by Tim Costello in another chapter of *Why Christianity Matters*, illustrated by the parable of *The Good Samaritan* the duty of Christians is to help and protect the marginalised and the dispossessed. Costello writes, "In Matthew 25, Jesus instructs His followers to care for the hungry, thirsty, homeless, naked, sick, and imprisoned – the marginalised, in whom His face can be revealed".

The reality is whether social welfare, health, aged care, or schools – religious-inspired and managed organisations like charities are a critical part of Australian society and our way of life. Without them, governments would find it impossible to cope. Martyn Iles makes a related point Christian virtues and beliefs strengthen community cohesion, reciprocity, and social capital.

One of the other authors contributing to *Christianity Matters*, Peter Craven, details how impoverished and threadbare Western culture would be without Christian-inspired literature, music, art, and architecture.

Craven writes, "The New Testament is part of the air we breathe, and may it ever be" and "When we stare at the Sistine Chapel ceiling or listen to Mozart's *Requiem* or his *Coronation Mass* we are not experiencing the rhetoric of a religious vision but an essence where beauty and truth are at one".

JRR Tolkien states the much applauded and popular *Lord of the Rings* trilogy is imbued with Christian concepts including the fight between good and evil, sin and redemption, and the struggle to resist temptation and instead do what is good. CS Lewis' *Narnia* books can also only be properly appreciated through a Christian perspective.

One of the other authors to *Christianity Matters*, Cardinal George Pell, in arguing the need to acknowledge and celebrate the word of God quotes from Solzhenitsyn, who realised communism was inherently nihilistic and evil and Christianity was the only viable alternative.

After referring to *The Gulag Archipelago*, Cardinal Pell writes, "He believed that the disasters of twentieth century Russian history occurred because 'men have forgotten God'; indeed, he sees this as 'the principal trait of the entire twentieth century'".

Former Prime Minister, John Howard, in a speech to young liberals wisely argued:

> *Any party which seeks to have a long period in government, any party that seeks to maintain its relevance to the Australian community, will always be a party both of ideas and ideals… A political party that does not give pride of place to ideals and values is a political party that will very quickly lose not only its soul but also its sense of direction.*

Conclusion

One of the defining characteristics of civilised societies is the ability to think clearly and to weigh arguments and debates in a logical and rational way. While emotion plays its part, more important is the ability to be impartial and objective.

It is also critical words have agreed meanings and language is not used to unduly influence and control how individuals conceptualise, think and communicate. As noted by Orwell, one of the most frightening things is when totalitarian regimes, either of the left or the right, use language to indoctrinate people and enforce mind control and group think.

One of the early arguments used to defend political correctness is that it's wrong to use language to unfairly discriminate against or stigmatise people because of who or what they are. There's no doubt many of the words used to describe homosexuals, women, Asians, Aborigines and black Americans were, and still are, offensive and unacceptable.

It is also true society was structured in such a way that not all were treated equally or fairly and more needed to be done to address unconscious bias and structural discrimination. During the 60s and 70s feminists had every right to argue women needed greater freedom in what was a society characterised by male dominance.

At the same time, over the last 30 or so years there is no doubt political correctness, rebadged as being Woke, has been weaponised to such a degree that it represents an existential threat to Western societies like Australia. Such is the extreme nature of Woke ideology that rationality and reason no longer prevail. Instead, arguments and debate are settled by appeal to emotion and what individuals *feel* is correct and beyond doubt.

A feminist questioning whether a man can be a woman is immediately condemned as a transgender exclusive radical feminist (TERF), argue the benefits of Western civilisation and you are guilty of white supremacism and if you suggest multiculturalism is flawed you will be attacked as xenophobic and racist.

On university campuses trigger warnings, safe spaces and diversity and inclusivity guidelines cocoon students in a Woke echo chamber ensuring their beliefs are never questioned or challenged. Courses of study are structured to ensure the prevailing cultural-left orthodoxy dominates and any academics who fail to conform are no-platformed, fail to get promoted or are cancelled.

The danger, if rationality, reason and impartial disagreement and debate are rendered impossible, is the only alternatives are violence or epistemological suicide. Equally as concerning, illustrated by Victoria's lockdown during the Covid-19 epidemic, is hard fought for freedoms and liberties are easily erased when demagogues like Dictator Dan prevail.

Woke ideology, in claiming the First Fleet was an invasion, Australian history is one of exploitation, genocide and racism and there is nothing beneficial or worthwhile about Western civilisation is also committing cultural suicide. By cancelling the nation's patrimony succeeding generations of young Australians have nothing to be proud of and are destined to cultural illiteracy.

Wokeness, underpinned as it is by cultural-Marxism, is also a deeply secular, materialistic ideology that ignores the importance of a spiritual, transcendent view of the world and the need to be morally grounded. Not surprisingly, Australia has one of the highest rates of anxiety, depression, self-harm and drug abuse as there is nothing providing a deeper and more lasting sense of meaning and nourishing the soul.

Over the long course of history it's true societies evolve and change over time. History also tells us even in the darkest hours, the innate thirst for reason, rationality and the need to commit to the common good and human flourishing prevail. Recent events, including the 60/40 No vote to the Voice referendum, the increasing suspicion and push back against Woke ideology and parents and teachers starting their own classical, liberal/arts schools, suggest the pendulum is moving back to sanity and common sense.

www.ingramcontent.com/pod-product-compliance
Lightning Source LLC
Chambersburg PA
CBHW072129020426
42334CB00018B/1725